FAITH:
MY WALKING CANE TO GLORY

A NOVEL BY
DELOIS JACKSON

DORRANCE PUBLISHING CO., INC.
PITTSBURGH, PENNSYLVANIA 15222

ISBN # 0-8059-5937-8

Printed in the United States of America

First Printing
For information or to order additional books, please write:
Dorrance Publishing Co., Inc.
643 Smithfield Street
Pittsburgh, Pennsylvania 15222
U.S.A.
1-800-788-7654
Or visit our web site and on-line catalog at www.dorrancepublishing.com

"PRAYER"

"Father, in the name of Jesus, I come to you this day as humble as I know how. As I go into this prayer, Lord, I bring Your presence with me. I acknowledge You in all my ways, all my thoughts, all my decisions, and thanking you for all of my many blessings, and accomplishments. Father, I come with Thanksgiving in my heart. I come to you because there is no other name that I can call upon and there is nowhere else I can go. Lord, I ask that you cast out hate and replace it with love. Lord, if there is something that is in our lives that is not pleasing to You, please move it. Make us vessels, Lord, that you can use. Lord, give us that loving spirit, that forgiving spirit in the name of Jesus. Father, we thank you for forgiving us for all of our many sins and throwing them into the sea of forgetfulness. We thank you for helping us to be able to forgive the ones who trespass against us; because Lord, we know that in order for You to forgive us, we must be able to forgive our enemies. Lord, I am praying for the salvation of all the sinners out there today. Lord, lead and guide our young people; and give them wisdom and understanding. Strengthen their parents and guide them in raising their children in the way they should go. In the book of Proverbs, You said to, "Train up a child in the way he should go: and when he is old, he will not depart from it." Lord Jesus, I ask in your strong name that you continue to order my steps in your Words because; You said that the steps of a good man are ordered by You. Lord, I don't want to walk this journey alone. Lord, I bless your Holy name; I give you the highest praise— Hallelujah, hallelujah, hallelujah! Lord, I will honor you and bless you at all times; Your praises shall continually be in my mouth. I am praying for those who are seeking your Kingdom. My prayer is that these inspiring words will encourage every reader to spend time with You so as to allow you to strength their heart and to show them the importance of abiding in Your Son Jesus Christ."

Author: DeLois Jackson

"SPECIAL DEDICATION"

A very special dedication to my dearest and loving mother, Annie Jackson, who gave me life; and departed this life just as I was finishing the writing of this novel. It is truly a joy and indeed a great pleasure to honor you with this novel. You were a wonderful mother, the best any child could ever hope for. I can't begin to tell you how blessed I felt to be one of your thirteen children. I dedicate this novel to you. Without you, it would not have been possible for me to write such an awesome inspirational book to encourage others to hold on and not give up. I thank you for all that you did for me. Most importantly, I thank you for the Love that you so generously gave to me down through the years, and the faith that you instilled so deeply in me. I love you and will forever cherish the relationship we had.

"DEDICATION"

To my wonderful family, especially my three beautiful daughters, Tonya, Adora and NaKisha, who went through all the struggles and strains with me—the good, the bad and the ugly, I also dedicate this novel to you. Girls—I know that God is blessing our family through all of our trials and tribulations but the best is yet to come. You are the best gifts that anyone could ever possibly dream of having. I did not know when God blessed me to become pregnant with each of you, that you would change my life forever—and contributed to the inspiration I received from God to deliver this novel of sermons and messages.

However, I must say, initially I was very disappointed in myself for getting pregnant; but, my daughters made it all worthwhile and they forever changed my life for the better; because, the first look at each of them gave me all the motivation and inspiration I needed to show the world that they were not mistakes. They were "the perfect gifts" from God. It was them who gave me the determination and the zeal in which I needed to be molded into what I have become today. It was all because they were worth the sacrifice. Not only did God graciously bless me with them, but He also blessed the whole world with each of them to share in their lives, their beautiful smile and also to spread the joy that they bring with such lovely smile. I wanted them to have the very best that life had to offer. If God had not blessed me with them, I would not know how to appreciate Him for so many other wonderful blessings He has so graciously bestowed upon me.

"ACKNOWLEDGEMENT"

To God—I thank you! I give you all the glory, honor, and praise for inspiring me, and giving me the Will to write these words of inspiration.

I offer my gratitude to my husband, family and friends for their love, support and encouragement to take this enormous step to embark upon such a journey to inspire others.

Thanks to Debra Judkins, a lady whom I met on the airplane, New Years Eve, 1998, who prayed with me and for me; and asked God to anoint this book so that when it is read, lives will be touched. Thanks to Lena Huntley for her very encouraging words and votes of confidence in me.

I'd like to personally thank every one of you for your prayers, guidance, and best wishes; and for sharing such a wonderful blessing and experience with me. I will always appreciate each of you for your love, support, and most importantly, encouragement that you have given, which can never be expressed in words.

Always providing words of enhancement, wisdom, and continues to provide constructive criticism. I like to thank my personal editor, Barbara Johnson, author of two published novels, "Chinaberry Lane", Elizabeth M. Singleton, (*nom de plume*) and "A Mississippi Family", who was quite patient with me while I embarked upon my writing adventure. For many months before I met her I worked feverishly compiling my manuscript for a book. However, she looked it over and told me that it needed much more work before publishing and that I might want to keep the first marked-up editing draft as a souvenir to look back on to see how far I had come and how much I had grown and expanded from. I wanted to crawl under a big rock and cry. Tears of disappointment streaked down my cheeks because I thought about the amount of time I had spent writing this book, and my faith was telling me that it had to be "a best seller", but then she told me that my book needed much more work. Then, she told me later that she hoped I understand and appreciate the complexity of such editing because this is how masterpieces are made. At that point, I started to feel somewhat better about what I had embarked upon because I knew that I had something great, "A Masterpiece" for everybody to read, enjoy and be inspired. Thank God for being my solid rock of strength on which my faith stands firmly on.

Finally, I would like to thank Dorrance Publishing Company and all of its staff for treating this novel of inspiration with the utmost integrity and dignity.

FAITH:
MY WALKING CANE
TO GLORY

TABLE OF CONTENT

INTRODUCTION

From a young girl growing up in Northwest Florida, playing on the streets between the cities of Crestview and Fort Walton Beach, with my sisters and brothers, I have always wanted to do something special to help people. I am the twelfth child of thirteen children. There were eight daughters and five sons—and I am the seventh daughter.

As I often gazed out of the window, looking up toward heaven, listening to the birds sang so beautifully, flowers blooming all around me in so many various colors, different types, and the aroma from the different fragrances, I began dreaming and hoping that one day I would grow up to become someone very special and great—someone to be remembered. That one amazing image of what God allowed me to glimpse and enjoy for just a few moments while I gazed out of the window was worth more than a thousand pictures—no artist on this side of heaven could ever paint a picture more beautifully, nor could they paint it more vividly. This is when the true meaning of who I wanted to become came into focus. I began cultivating my dreams from that moment.

During the summers, with the temperature ranging anywhere from 90 degrees to slightly over a 100 degrees, we would quench our thirst with a big glass of Kool-Aid, or some good ole cold ice tea. Another great memory of summer in Northwest Florida was eating a big bowl full of ice milk—we couldn't afford ice cream—so our treat was ice milk. Hi-C sodas and moon pies were also great favorites of ours. Other memories of ours were when we would set on the porch taking in the nice cool breeze from the wind and the shade from the big trees, surrounding our home, and talk about old times. Also, playing checkers with a friend or older family members, like my favorite uncle who thought that he was the best checker player in the whole world.

I grew up in a Baptist church where I served as a member of the junior usher board, junior missionary society, and participated in Christmas and Easter programs. I attempted to sing in the junior choir knowing that I could not hold a note, not even a handwritten note, if someone had passed me one; I couldn't pass it on to the next person, that is just how bad my singing really is—off beat and totally out of rhythm.

I have always had a great compassion and concern for people. If they were in need of something—anything, it didn't matter, I tried to help provide that need and encouraged them to hold on because I felt that a change would eventually come and change their situation for the better. Sometimes listening was all the help they really needed and usually, it was all they wanted in order to feel better about their situation, and about themselves.

Nonetheless, each day I played with my dolls, jacks and ball, yo-yos, hula-hoops and ric rack sets. I even played hopscotch and marbles. Although, I was kept busy with my many activities, the desire to help people grew stronger and stronger. I believe that it grew stronger because I was left at home a lot as a child while my mother worked day and night with two and three jobs for as long as I could remember to ensure that we had the basic things in life—food, clothes, and shelter. I also remembered the discipline we got when we disobeyed my mother's house rules. She would remind us every now and then not to get to big for our britches—we knew exactly what she meant when she used the term "don't get to big for your britches", because the next thing you knew, you would be getting a whipping.

Little did I know as a child how God would use me to help touch, inspire and encourage other people to hold-on until their change comes. He has allowed me to experience and endure so many bumps, trials, tribulations, pain, heartaches and headaches in my life. I can only hope and pray by writing this book, some of my experiences or something will be written to inspire and encourage someone else to make a difference in their life—to lighten some of their burdens. Also, to let them know that they are not going through their troubles alone because other people have been down that very same road before. When I thought about all the things that I had gone through, and all the things that God had brought me out of, I just knew that God had a great plan for my life. I just did not know exactly what He had in mind but I had a good feeling that one day He was going to use me as one of His vessels.

Each day that I walk with God—He is helping me to become a better person; He improves upon my character and is constantly carving off things that are not pleasing to Him. I believe that He is making me a good woman, a good wife, a good mother and no doubt, a good Christian.

This book was written first as a therapist with conviction that's encouraging, uplifting and inspiring. It was also written to create a forum by which to share information while motivating others as well as to offer hope and entertainment for people who are in need of being inspired, uplifted and encouraged to bring about a change in their life. It will offer you comfort to use as you minister to the spiritual needs of people struggling with life's adversities. I have always aspired to do something along the lines of spreading the "good news." What better way to spread the "good news"—God's words—than to put it into a book for many to read?

This is an inspirational book that will hopefully feed the soul, and prayerfully, it will lead people to Christ. It will also foster Christian growth and Godliness. This book will focus on acts of faith. It will further discuss heritages from the Lord; overcoming life's adversities; folding the napkin on things that keep us from developing a spiritual relationship and hindering us from getting closer to God; making the right choice to live for Christ; to having a personal encounter with angels, God's messengers; counting our blessings as God has blessed us abundantly; to triumphs over tribulations; to reaping the rewards of faith; to soaring to new heights; to discovering our true destiny in Christ; to personal testimonies to encourage and inspire others to allow God to walk with them through this life's journey; and wrapping it up with FAITH: My Walking Cane To Glory. I will further use some of my personal experiences to lend some credence and my personality to the piece. I consider the targeted audience to be people in need of God's love, support, and spiritual guidance.

The word of God tells us to, "Seek ye first, the Kingdom of God and His righteousness, and all of these things shall be added unto you." God said He would give us all our hearts desires just for seeking Him first and His righteousness. Approximately eight years ago in 1994, I had a desire to write a book. However, at that time, I did not have a title for a book, nor did I have the words to put into one. I just had a desire. By seeking God's guidance first, and His righteousness, on January 2, 1998, while sitting in the den of my home, in Montgomery, Alabama, with my husband, an overwhelming feeling came over me, the Holy Spirit spoke and said, "write a book." I told my husband what had just happened to me, he said, "let's go to store and get a notebook so you can start jotting down your thoughts." So, up off the couch and to the store we went.

I said, Wow!

Me! Write a book!

On what, "I asked"?

The Holy Spirit said, on "Faith."

I said, "on Faith"?

The title of the book was conceived at that moment and I gave it the subtitle of "My Walking Cane to Glory." I gave it, "My Walking Cane To Glory" because through all of my troubles, trials and tribulations, Faith has truly been my walking cane without it, I don't know where I would be; it's been leading and guiding me everyday through this life's journey. God gave me the desires of my heart, and as you can see, my book has been written, and the rest is history.

CHAPTER ONE
ABOUT FAITH

Faith, as you know, has several different definitions and descriptions. However, it is defined in my bible as the substance of things hoped for and the evidence of things not seen (KJV Heb 11:1). Webster defines faith as allegiance to duty or a person—*loyalty*; belief and trust in and loyalty to God; and a firm belief in something for which there is no proof; complete trust and also, it is something that is believed with strong conviction—a system of religious beliefs.

Faith is no more than trusting, and believing that God will bring our situation to pass. Faith can be identified as the actual relationship that exists between the believer and God. The relationship between God and each individual who has dared to trust God despite what may be touched, seen, heard, or tasted—all of the material stuff. No matter what you are going through, have enough faith in God and wait patiently on Him and He will fix the problem for you.

Furthermore, faith is a belief based on past experiences that God's new and fresh surprises would surely one day be ours. Having confidence in God and being sure of whom we are in Christ describe our faith. Certainty in Christ shows how strong we are when trials come our way. We must believe in God's character—He is who He says He is. Also, we must believe in God's promises—He will do what He says He will do. Faith is also one of the characteristics of God. It is one of the fruit of the Spirit. Faith is dependable, it's loyal and it's stable. You can't be wishy-washy when it comes to God's business. Great is your faithfulness.

Moreover, faith is total dependence on God. It's a desire and a willingness to do His Will. It is the foundation for the Christian life, and it is the means by which all unseen things are tested. Faith means trust and confidence in what God has promised us. It is not something that one uses to put on a show or an act for others to see. Faith is complete and humble obedience to God's Word and to His Will, and the readiness to do whatever He calls us to do. God wants us to be willing vessels to do His Will because He does not want us to do anything for Him grudgingly. The amount or quantity of faith is not as important as the right kind or quality of faith—faith in our all-powerful God is the kind of faith we want to have.

The bible tells me that there are many different kinds of faith. The Bible talks about doctrinal faith that refers to the content of Christian belief. Saving faith is when we trust in Christ and in Him alone for our salvation. Justifying faith is where the believer relies solely on the fact that God has declared him righteous. Indwelling faith, on the other hand, is trusting God's Word in and through us—we no longer live so that Christ can live in us. Daily faith is that day-to-day dependence on God which is all part of the sanctification process.

Faith can produce personal deliverance and sometimes it can even produce societal deliverance. You must first have Hope because Hope is the partner to Faith. Faith makes us sure of what we hope for and gives us proof of what we cannot see. It is because of our faith that we know that the world was made at God's command. We also know what can be seen was made out of what cannot be seen.

Further, we must go from faith to faith and from glory to glory striving for the Mark of the high calling. God said in His words that the "just shall live by faith." Faith is an essential attribute of God. By no means did man invent faith. It was truly God's revelation. I believe if faith were left up to man, he never would have thought of it. It's too great of an imagination for man to comprehend. Also, if we believe the gospel according to God, we will have everlasting life with Him. Otherwise, we will have death and be separated from God. What good does it do us to say we have faith when we do nothing to show that we truly have faith? Also, we say we trust in God with all our heart, yet we continue to strive to solve our own situations without Him. That is not the kind of faith that can save us? Anybody who doesn't breathe is dead, and faith that is weak and does nothing to include God wholeheartedly is just as dead! God dealt to every man and woman a measure of faith and it is what we do with the faith that makes us who we become.

God doesn't want us to think too highly of ourselves; but He does want us to be honest in evaluating our self-worth in who we have become in Christ because apart from Him—we are nothing but filthy rags! We are not capable of very much by eternal standards—in Him, we are very valuable and we are capable of worthy service. It is according to our faith as to how God elevates us from level to level. "Faith is what we believe on the inside, which is an inward confidence, a happy spirit, and a peaceful heart that is manifested by an outward action or result."

It is through much prayer and supplication that we see how strong our faith is in God. Also, as we mature and grow in Christ, we see how prayer and fasting change our situations and how easy it is to give our problems over to God and leave them there with Him. Our love for God is shown through our faith in Him—believing and trusting Him to take care of our needs. Faith must grow in us and while faith is growing in us, Christ also grows in us. Just as the branches cannot bear fruit unless it shares the life of the living vine, we can produce nothing unless we continue to grow spiritually in Christ—studying His words daily. Faith teaches us that the more we know about God's word, the more we grow spiritually. Faith is our security in knowing Christ. Faith is the path to success. Faith and perseverance were the thresholds to the many opportunities that life has to offer. Faith truly provides the key to unlock the doors of opportunities. It provided the key to a better life for me as a young mother.

We must feed our faith with the word of God to grow in Christ, and perish doubt by believing that God can and will allow our dreams and goals to come to past. If you desire to have something, it can be achieved or accomplished. The desire to achieve something carries with it the necessary knowledge, skills and ability to accomplish it. If you can truly believe that your hopes and dreams are attainable, that is the first step in conceiving and achieving your dreams; because, if you can conceive your dreams, you can achieve them by pursuing them one step at a time. Because through hard work, perseverance and faith, you can do anything you desire. God says that, *"We can do all things through Christ Jesus who strengthens us."* We feed our faith by reading the scriptures and believing in God's word. When we step out on faith, we believe that God is truly going to manifest and bring that belief to past. "If it is a blessing or a dream from God, it will definitely be impossible, impractical and imperative for man to understand or comprehend; because, we can not see with our natural eyes how it can possibly materialize." To believe that you can do it, and that it is possible for you to attain it, is just as equal in importance to your desire. A person normally won't work on a goal without believing that it is achievable or attainable, and belief in it motivates you to success. You need to nurture your belief. Unlike desires that seem to appear in our minds automatically, belief needs nurturing. Doubts have a way of creeping in—along with all the negative vibes we receive from others, often times, including our very close friends and family. Because you need to nurture your faith, to believe in yourself, you need to have an understanding of how to build your self-confidence. If you don't nurture your belief, your achievement momentum will be stopped. It is hard to work toward a goal when your mind is full of all the reasons why 'you' can't do it.

There are a few ways and approaches for developing faith in yourself and in God, which is necessary to accomplish your spiritual freedom and anything else you so desire. By having faith in yourself and in the Almighty God, you will be able to fulfill your dreams—whatever your dreams maybe, you will be able to accomplish them. Your dreams or desires maybe to become a better Christian, or perhaps, advancement in your career. One way is to develop belief in yourself and in the goals that you have set. Also, look into all aspects of your goals and dreams to see where you are headed. You must be able to see your dreams—visualizing will help to achieve your results. Self-visualization is so very important to see where you are going and where you are going to end up. See if your goals or dreams are obtainable—can it be done. Keep a positive attitude at all times while achieving your dreams. Dreams start by visualizing what you want, asking God to guide you, then seeing yourself achieving that goal. Visualization is a way and a process by which to began achieving your goals and dreams in life. The confidence level you need to be successful will begin to develop, grow and materialize with your faith in God, then in yourself.

Constantly visualize yourself successfully achieving your goals or dreams. If your desire is strong enough and you truly believe that you can achieve it, you are already half way to being successful—then He will take you the rest of the way.

Another way is to visualize yourself not just achieving them, but already in possession of your goals or dreams. Look at yourself in a positive way. Success is for you just as well as it is for others. Don't put limitations on yourself.

Lastly, just try to do it—try to achieve your goals or dreams. The best way to build faith in yourself, and in your ability to accomplish your dreams, or anything else, is to do it—start taking steps towards getting it done. Dreams are achieved by making progress one-step at a time—little by little. One of the most important steps in achieving your dream is to try it, because if you don't ever try to do it, you'll never know if you can do it, if you don't get some practical experience. Your confidence level and faith are both built from positive experiences. Success is a process. As a reminder for us to keep reaching for the Mark of the High calling, we need to keep the faith and continue to trust in God to get us there. God said, "Be faithful until death, and I will give you the crown of life." (Revelation 2:10). Faithfulness is a manifestation of the fruit of the spirit that pertains to loyalty and trustworthiness. Trust God to guide you through your successes—allow Him to be your walking cane to glory.

People just like you and me build great achievements day-by-day, step-by-step. Greatness comes from ordinary people and their actions, focused on a specific objective or goal, followed by or with steadfastness and resolve. Better yet, every year we resolve to setting New Year's resolutions, such as setting out to loose weight, eating healthier and exercising more; but yet somewhere between the middle and the end of the year, we drop the ball in achieving these goals. But, through Christ Jesus, anything and everything is possible when we are dedicated and committed to pursuing our dreams and goals one step at a time. The bottom line here is, if our desire is strong enough, we must trust and believe that God will empower and equip us to obtain our desires. We must have a healthy and positive attitude, and the faith to know that God is working on our behalf.

Also, our attitudes are capable of determining where we will go in life, whether we will go ahead or withdraw, if we will persevere or quit, if we will remain open to new opportunities and ideas or will we just continue to be complacent and just remain frozen in our past. Attitudes are like viruses; they could be very contagious. Is your attitude worth catching? If not, you may want to consider changing it to a more positive one because we wouldn't want to pass around our rotten, stinking and contagious attitudes.

When we believe and when we have hope in God, that He will fulfill His promises even though we don't see those promises materializing, we demonstrate true faith.

Salvation is ours just for the asking. Salvation should be every Christian's destiny. It means total deliverance. The ultimate salvation will be when we as Christians will be rescued from the world into the presence of God. If you want to grow in Christ, you must first confess your sins and believe in your heart that God has raised Jesus from the dead, and you shall be saved—that's a promise from God. We don't have to do anything special because we are saved by God's grace through faith which is no works of our own, it is not as a result of any effort, ability, intelligent choice, or act of service on our part; it is truly a gift from God (Ephesians 2:8). By reasons of, both salvation and faith are gifts from the Lord; we should constantly have thanksgiving in our hearts and be on our knees with gratitude, praise and joy.

Remember, once we are saved, we are not saved merely for our own benefit or edification; but, to serve Him; build up the church by helping to bring others to Christ. Also, out of gratitude for the gifts that God has deposited in us, we should seek to help and serve others with kindness, charity, and goodness. Whether our gifts are in writing, inspiring, encouraging others, or just loving our neighbor as ourselves, we should be grateful to God for He is the one who blesses us with our many gifts and talents. The word of God tells us to be faithful. God is looking for faithfulness but He wants us faithfully to help Him do His job, because if we don't He just might find someone else to do it in our place.

Furthermore, when we look back on where God has brought us from to where we are today, we know that it is by Faith in God and God's faithfulness to us that we've come this far—by leaning and depending on the Lord. We must constantly remember that our Faith is tested daily and every time God brings us through these tests, it teaches us to trust Him just a little bit more, in turn, strengthening our faith and making us more stronger, physically and spiritually.

God has ways of teaching us about faith and how to grow stronger in our faith, through life's experiences as well as through His words and those who are inspired to write them. God also tells us that without Faith, it is impossible to please Him. No matter what, we must believe that God has our best interest at heart. He will not steer us in the wrong direction. Without Faith works is dead. God tells us to lean not unto our own understanding, but in all of our ways to acknowledge Him and He will direct our path (Proverbs 3:5).

Ultimately, faith comes by hearing and hearing comes from the word of God. He tests our faith through trials and tribulations. He wants to see how well we handle the situations that he puts us in—do we really trust Him enough to bring us out of our troubles. We must walk the walk, and talk the talk because it goes hand-in-hand with each other. For example, we must pray and tell other people that God was pierced in the side for our transgressions, utterly crushed for our iniquities, the chastisement of our peace was upon Him, and with His stripes we are healed, when they get sick. We must truly believe that He will also heal our bodies when it becomes afflicted and racked with pain. Being healed actually refers to our spiritual condition being made whole with God. We can't doubt God's Word and expect healing in our bodies. God said that we are to walk by faith and not by sight. Faith has to overcome doubt. Faith will also restore our belief and confidence in ourselves and in God through Jesus Christ. All we need is a tiny mustard seed of faith.

A mustard seed is very small; but it is alive and it will grow, granted, if it is planted and cultivated over time. Faith in God is like a tiny seed, a small amount of it will take root and grow when we ensure that it's planted in the right place. At first, you can hardly see it, and then it will begin to spread underground and then visibly. Although each change will be gradual and imperceptible, soon with the proper nourishing this faith will have produced major results that will eventually uproot and destroy competing loyalties. As often heard, we don't need more faith because that tiny seed of faith is just enough if it is alive and growing. All we need to do is to continue to keep it cultivated by keeping it watered and fertilized with the Word of God. Although prayer is the key to the Kingdom, we must have faith—because faith is the key to unlock the door to the Kingdom. The word of God also tells us that, "if ye had faith as a grain of mustard seed, ye might say unto the sycamine tree, be thou planted in the sea; and it shall obey you." (KJV Luke 17:6). Faith has got me covered, and as long as I've got a little bit of faith in me—God's got me in the palms of His hands and He will continue to keep me covered and protected in this life and beyond.

CHAPTER TWO
HERITAGES FROM THE LORD

Unless we have God's blessing, every human effort is in vain. If we want eternal life and everlasting blessings while we live, we must rely on God to give them to us. Life without God and faith in Him is senseless. All of our life's work, building our dream homes, establishing our careers, and raising our families, must have God as the foundation to keep it all together and to keep it from falling. God said in His words that "Children are a heritage of the Lord, and the fruit of the womb is His reward."

I became a mother very early in my life, however, reflecting back to that time in my life, I do not look at my pregnancies as mistakes; because in my opinion, God does not make mistakes. A mistake is something that you can go back and correct. A mistake can be erased and you can start all over again. You cannot correct a miracle that God blesses you with and that's exactly what a life is—a miracle, and only God should be able to take it away. Besides aborting an infant, how can you correct a pregnancy—You can't! Also, a child isn't a thing or an object that you can put on a shelf, wait until it turns eighteen years old, go back to pick it up and decide, suddenly, that you want to become a mother—that's too late. The child has grown up and has developed into a young adult. You are a parent for the long haul unless you give it up for adoption. Mothers, if you want to be blessed, love your children as God has loved you; nurture your children as God has instructed you to do. If you are struggling and straining to support your children, keep your children with you, and don't pass them off on other people to do the job that God has charged you to do. By keeping the children with you while you are going through your troubles allows them to see how you handle life's situation and overcome the obstacles in your life. It will help to mold and shape them at an early stage in their life which could help them grow and understand some of life's expectancies before they are forced to have to face the world and make decision on their own. It will help them to be more responsible and accountable for their actions. You will be blessed for not treating your heritage as an inconvenience. They are gifts from God and should be treated as such.

The greatest responsibility God gives a parent is the nurturing and guidance of their children. We must love them, cherish them and honor them as God has directed us to do. God tells us that we as parents are responsible to train up our children in the way they should go, and when they grow older they will not depart from what they were taught. We as parents are to lay the foundation of faith in living before them as Christians, honoring God, and under girding them with prayer and polishing them with the teaching of God's Word. We should never devalue our children because when we do, we cross swords with God almighty. Children are truly our rewards and heritages from the Lord. It is through Christ Jesus that little children are blessed. In the book of Mark, it talks about how we should allow little children to come to God and forbid them not. Jesus stated, "Verily I say unto you, Whosoever shall not receive the kingdom of God as a little child, he shall not enter therein." God charged parents to raise their children in a respectable, Christian, and loving environment. We as parents are to teach our children the way of the Lord while they are yet young giving them an opportunity to receive the Kingdom of God.

There are many ways by which we inherit God's kingdom and earthly blessings—one way is through our off-springs. My daughters are wonderful blessings to me. They are very special in many ways, and they are my rewards—my heritage from the Lord, bringing me much joy and happiness. I also found God through my daughters, because of their disobedience, they kept me on my knees praying to the Lord, and one day, the Lord heard my cry and gave me a peace of mind that remains with me to this day. That to me is very special and sacred. Thanks girls, without you I might still be lost in the wilderness.

Rearing children is a sacred responsibility and as parents, we must depend on the Lord to help us raise our children. We should have willing attitudes and do everything in our home with honor and pleasure because we are doing it for the rewards and blessings that God has given us. He gave us our children to love and to nurture. During their teenage years, my children didn't appear to be that special, because all I could think about was the heartaches and pains they were causing. Initially, I didn't believe my daughters were truly blessings from God; because blessings are suppose to be good and not be painful or hurtful, but, God wanted us to grow spiritually as a family, and beyond our pains and sorrows. Through all the pains and sorrows, God was teaching us a lesson on how to love unconditionally. Agape love! Agape love is amazing! Agape love is astounding! Agape love is selfless! Agape love is what God has for us and wants us to have for other people. It is self-starting and compassionate. Agape love is constant, and it never changes. It is immeasurable and voluntary. Nobody has to make you love because it will come naturally. Agape love is a gift from God, and it will cause us to respond lovingly to one another in times of need. Agape love will have you apologizing when you really don't want to. Agape love moves grudges.

Although I was a very young mother, I matured quickly and became the best little mom in my community. So that my children had what they needed at all times, I sacrificed buying clothes for myself, didn't go out to eat a lot and many material items I wanted I didn't get until my daughters left home. Trips and many other nice to have things were only a dream. I was determined that my children would not need for a thing because it was my responsibility to

ensure that their needs were met in every possible way—be it spiritually, physically, emotionally or materially. I wanted them to know, as their mother, that
they were safe and secure with me. I also wanted them to know that I would
not leave them for anyone, anybody or anything, no matter what we were
going through because I was blessed to bring them into this world. I would not
want someone else to do the job that the Lord had blessed me to do—which
was to be their mother and raise my wonderful children. I was able to raise
them by trusting in God, leaning and depending on Him; and having complete
faith that He would watch over my three lovely daughters and me during that
stage of our lives.

Take a look at some of the people that are around you everyday who are
healthy, financially stable and able to have and raise children and they cannot
even conceive the miraculous heritage from the Lord—His great heritage and
blessings of having children.

Children are too often seen as liabilities rather than assets. But the Bible
calls children "an heritage of the Lord,"—a reward. We can learn so many valuable lessons from their inquisitive minds and trusting spirits. Those of you who
view children as a distraction or nuisance should, instead, see them as an
opportunity to shape the world and the future, even to find cures for the
world's deadly diseases, such as AIDS, cancer, asthma, tuberculosis, diabetes,
and others. We dare not treat our precious children—God's wonderful gifts, as
an inconvenience, a burden, or hindrance when God blesses us with this heritage and He values them so highly. So, I know that my three daughters were
truly a blessing, a miracle from God to carry on my life. Thank you Lord!

My daughters have brought me so much joy and happiness, and through
them, my faith in God has also grown much stronger; but one of the hardest
things I ever had to do was to watch my daughters grow up making mistakes
that they had to live with for the rest of their lives and I couldn't do anything
about it; but, trust God to fix the problems and bring them out of their situations victoriously.

When I think about the joy and happiness in my life—my mind quickly
takes me back to my daughters. There are days when I will reflect back over my
life, and think about some of the things that they use to do, and it will either
put a smile on my face, or bring tears to my eyes. I often think about the many
mementos my daughters gave to me, hand made for me, or bought for me for
all of those very special occasions—Birthdays, Mother's Day, Valentine's Day,
Christmas and they would also give me gifts just for being me—their mom. I
remember when my oldest daughter made me a purple lollypop made out of
wood and shaped in the form of a heart, with the words, *"I love you mom"* written on one side, and the other side just had "from Tonya", on it. It is the
thought that counts the most. The lollypop currently sits on my desk as a constant reminder of the love, joy and happiness they bring into my life. Other
treasures they made for me were a pet frog, a pet rock, a strawberry painted on
a walnut, beautiful cards, inspiring letters, clothes, scented candles, many
poems written just for me, and just a wall full of plaques telling me how much
that I am loved and other treasures that bless my soul everyday because they

are so inspiring. I also recall when I gave my youngest daughter a car—a used car, a Toyota Corolla, for her high school graduation gift and she bought me a thank you card. Of course, like many other children, she had to add her little personal touch in the thank you note, by providing additional comments to the thank you card. In the notes she added, *"Mom, I just wanted you to know I really appreciate my car. Even though it is not what I'm use to driving, I still love it. I thank you for my car; but, I can't get use to reaching over the car to roll the windows up and down and having everything manually on it."* At the time, I was driving an Audi 5000, fully-loaded, with all the amenities of a luxury car, which she drove quite often prior to her getting her car.

One of my most memorable Mother's Day was when my daughters got together and wrote me a poem, presented little momentums. Each of them presented momentums based on their feelings of our relationship. The middle daughter gave me two flowers. A dead flower to represent the old daughter with the bad ways and the bad attitude. When I received the dead flower, I looked at it with a pause, wondering why I had received it.

"Why are you giving me a dead flower," I asked? "You must not have known it was dead when you bought it." She smiled! And, said, "Yes!" Then, she gave me a live flower. It was beautiful! It was also full of life. No brown, or dull looking leaves in sight. The live flower was to represent the new and improved daughter. She stated, "Mom, from now on, I'm going to change and start doing all the right things, the things I'm suppose to do and make you proud. I'm going to be a good mom to my children." These momentums may seem quite ordinary at first glance, but I treasure them all because when I think about where they came from and who gave them to me—my daughters, that makes it all so very special.

I was captivated by how all of the many gifts portrayed the concept of being connected to a living vine. I will keep the mementos as a reminder of the value of staying close to my daughters and to the Lord. I look at my daughters as branches off of my vine, my heritage from God. However, we are all branches to the true Vine of Jesus Christ, and we must stay firmly connected to that true Vine in order to mature into our full potential through Christ. Jesus is the True Vine and God is the gardener. If we are ever broken off from the Vine, we will wither away like grass, and we will soon die. God will cut away every branch of His that doesn't produce fruit. If a branch is simply near the Vine without being attached to it, it will never grow. It will eventually die. In order to produce fruit, the branch must remain united with the trunk. I thank God everyday for the lovely fruit that I was able to produce—my loving and thoughtful daughters who have produced and given me beautiful grandchildren. The key to fruit bearing is to stay connected to the true Vine who is again, Christ Jesus. The only way to be fruitful, and to be Christ-like, is to share with others, be it through gifts or just knowledge, as Christ did, stay united—stay connected to God—who is the true Vine.

CHAPTER THREE
OVERCOMING ADVERSITIES

God said in Isaiah that, "For my thoughts are not your thoughts, Nor are your ways my ways," says the Lord. For as the heavens are higher than the earth, so are My ways higher than your ways, and My thoughts than your thoughts."

I thank God everyday for not thinking like man thinks, and for using me to do His will—to use this dirty, broken, chipped, cracked and imperfect vessel for His purpose and for Him to be glorified.

A vessel is a hollow or concave utensil (i.e. a bottle, bowl, kettle, cup or a person) for holding something, or is used to navigate through water. Because I firmly believed that God could and would use broken and imperfect vessels, God is able to work through me to encourage and inspire others by navigating through life to reach those in need of His blessings and a stronger faith in Him. Now that God has transformed this cracked and imperfect vessel, He has begun a good work in my life.

A mother is the most important person in your life, the most influential person in your life, and only by the Grace of God, she gives you life. You respect everything about her. Also, you spend most of your life trying to please her because you care so much for her; you care about how she feels about you, and the choices that you make in life.

When I became pregnant, I had a minor set back and suddenly, life changed dramatically for me and took a turn for the worst. First, being pregnant out of wedlock was shocking and quite embarrassing. I also remembered the lack of sleep, low energy level and no real support from friends and family. I persevered and I continued to study and made sure that all of my homework was done and I also kept my grades up.

Just because you have children out of wedlock doesn't mean that you can't succeed and accomplish your dreams and goals. I thank God everyday for allowing us to make U-turns in the midst of our troubles in order to get back on the right track with Him, and overcome our many adversities. I was able to make life changing "U-turns" by discovering God's ability and His willingness to renew and rebuild my life. You can be assured that you will gain insight into your own faith walk from these intimate glimpses into my spiritual life, and hopefully you will be encouraged by some of my true-life stories.

At the age of 17, I found myself with two children and had not yet finished high school. However, I did not quit school, which my mother probably feared would happen; but I struggled through until I finished and received my diploma. After looking at the status of all my peers, I could see how she could have thought that I would have quit school, because many of the girls in my neighborhood got pregnant, quit school, started receiving welfare assistances and food stamps. After watching the patterns of the rest of my peers, my mother might have assumed that was going to be the way of life for me. Little did she know I had hope, dreams and goals.

About eight and a half months into my first pregnancy, my mother came home from work one very hot summer day, angry about something which to this day I still don't have a clue as to what had set her off and caused her to be so frustrated and angry. While sitting in the living room, I remember very vividly watching my mother get out of the car, walking across the grass, up the steps, and into the house. I was minding my own business, thinking to myself, *"how in the world did I let myself get into this mess—this situation"*, thinking about things that I needed to be doing for my soon-to-be newborn, watching the television, and eating watermelon. My mother walked through the door carrying several bags in her hands, with an angry, disgusted look on her face, she looked at me sitting there, and out of the blue—she called me a, "Big Old Mule," and said, "You Ain't Gonna be Nothing but Have a Bunch of Babies and be on Welfare for the Rest of Your Life!" At that instant, I slowly got up off the chair, put away the watermelon, and while struggling to hold back the tears from my eyes, I turned my back to her not wanting her to see how devastated and hurt I had become. It seemed as though, at that moment, all I could think of was that she must truly hate my guts; because not only had I embarrassed her by getting pregnant; but, also I was going to have extra baggage for her to care for. I felt as though I wanted to crawl up into a corner and just die because I had finally reached a fork in the road of no return, as far as my mother was concern. I truly felt as though I was at wits end, at the point of no return.

The words my mother spoke to me that day stabbed me in the heart like a knife. The words were so painful that they remained deep in my conscious mind and tortured me for many, many years afterwards. After speaking those hurtful words, it seemed to me that she had no remorse —no apologies—there was nothing. It was as though she didn't know that the words were stabbing comments that had penetrated my heart and conscious. Perhaps, she had a very frustrating time at work that day, and the sight of me being pregnant out of wedlock just set her off even more. I'm pretty sure now, like any other mother, she probably had great expectations for me, and some how, I failed her by getting pregnant out of wedlock.

For a while, I thought about mother's hurtful words daily. But, on the other hand, I couldn't do a thing about what she had said, nor could I turn back the hands of time and events that had led up to that day; but, I did pray and I would ask God continuously to bring me through the hurt victoriously. He did!

It is not enough to abstain from sharp words, petty contradictions, or daily little selfish cares. We must be active, honest and kind—not merely passive and unaffectionate. Hebrew 10:24 states, "Let us consider one another to provoke unto love and to good works." The bible also states that, "Ye fathers, provoke not your children to wrath: but bring them up in the nurture and admonition of the Lord." Basically, it means that we as parents can provoke our children to wrath by ridicule, cruelty and sometimes by abusing authority. We truly need to be careful how we treat our children because I personally believe that we can hinder some of our own blessings by how we treat our children—our gifts from God.

There is a lot of power in words, and we should be extremely careful about what we say to others and how we say it especially to those very close to us because, it could possibly devastate them for a lifetime. Words can destroy even the strongest person's character, their goals, their will to do good, their hopes and dreams if spoken or taken the way they weren't meant to be taken. When devastating and harsh words are spoken they are like witchcraft—like a curse to your soul. I could have been de-motivated to stop striving to reach my goals, dreams and continue to reach for the mark of the high calling, and to live up to God's expectations—and that could have been the death of my soul, my goals and my dreams had I been a weak person of poor faith and courage. Thank God for faith and the strength to endure the pain I felt.

Now that I am an adult, I am a parent, and after giving the situation some serious thought, I now believe that my mother felt as though I had let her down in some way by getting pregnant, and disobeying her will and wisdom about how hard life truly could be as a single parent—as she had experienced in raising all of us. Perhaps, from her viewpoint, I had fallen short of her expectation; because, I was no longer her little girl, in her eyes. I had become a grown-up because; in essence, I had done everything that she had done and was about to give birth to a baby. After all, she worked extremely hard everyday to insure that all of her children had all the necessary things in life—but then, her little girl was about to venture into some unchartered territory, having given birth to thirteen children, raising twelve of her own children and several grandchildren, she knew that I was not quite prepared to be a mother since I was merely a child myself.

My mother was the best mom anyone could ever have or ask for especially when we needed an ear or just someone to talk too. I don't believe that the comments were meant to be stabbing comments; I just believe that she had had an extremely bad day at work, and I was the next available person for her to vent out her frustration and anger on. However, this experience has taught me and helped me to understand how God expects us to do the right things, yet, as children not capable of using our better judgment, nor listen to Him, nor our parents, we often fall short of His expectations as well as our parents.

It was not until November 1993, over the Thanksgiving holiday, that I was able to confess to my mother that I'd remembered the statement she'd said to me many years ago when I was pregnant and what her words had done to me. Approximately 30 family members were visiting my home, in Montgomery, Alabama and during a moment of family confessions I was able to confess to her that she had said some very hurtful words to me. It had been twenty-three long years since she'd said those very painful words—twenty-three long years leading up to that day of the family confessions. The family confession wasn't planned, we were talking, and we started to reflect back over our lives, and talking about how far God had brought us. I just had to ask her if she had remembered saying those words to me, and when the moment finally came and I asked her, she said, "*no,*" she couldn't remember saying those painful words—but she didn't deny saying the words either. As I reminded her, her eyes got very teary, and she appeared to be somewhat surprised by the fact that I had mentioned it, or even remembered those hurtful words for twenty-three long years. However, the fact that she didn't realize saying the hurtful words, nor remembered that she had spoken such words hurt me even more. But, me having been in a predicament that made me an easy victim of her frustration and anger at the time, I recall being in a state of shock when she spoke them to me. I was numb and had become very angry. As my mother sat listening to me confess what I had kept hidden in my heart and soul all those years, I was even able to have enough courage to tell her in a moment of boldness that she was the reason I never got welfare, food stamps or even asked her for any type of support. I wanted to reveal to her what a little dose of faith in God and in myself had done for me, though; by no means, I never meant to be vengeance or hurt her in anyway, but only to confess and convey to her how such an adverse impact had really turned out positively. God said vengeance belongs to Him, that He would repay them.

During the time of my confession to my mother, while trying to hold back the tears from my own eyes, I noticed again that her eyes had gotten very watery too. Looking upon her in disbelief. Yet, the thought of it seemed to have sunk deeply into her heart, if not her memory. I was shocked! It was unbelievable that she could not recall having made such a statement. The fact that I carried that pain around for twenty-three long years, hurting daily, not knowing whether or not I would ever be able to tell her about it—to get it off my chest, she had already forgotten it, didn't even think about the painful words. That's why we need to be extremely careful about what we say to people because, if you are not strong in your faith, it truly could leave a devastating impact on your life. At that moment I felt the desire to embrace her; but at the same time, I felt that she needed those moments to reflect back for a moment and think about those painful words, and how damaging they could have been for me had I not been as strong as I was with enough wisdom to believe that I would overcome the adversities.

Reminding my mother of the pain I'd endured over the years from her wrath wasn't exactly the satisfaction I was seeking. Though, I felt that wall had to be broken down between her—I also wanted to open the pathway to an appreciation for her as I've always prayed my children would have for me in spite of the many adversities we had to overcome. This allows us to worship God in peace and attain spiritual freedoms like never before.

I also thought about all of the good things that she had done for me—the fact that she didn't kick me out of the house as a result of me getting pregnant was remarkable. She also clothed me, fed me, kept a roof over my head, we were never evicted from our home, and because of her love, and the values that she instilled in me—I was able to be a better mother to my own children. I was able to raise my daughters in a loving, caring, and Christian home, and also I was able to properly nurture them in becoming the respectful women that they are becoming today. Through those painful words that my mother spoke that day, I learned to be careful not to say painful and negative statements to my own children because of what it could have possibly done to their self-esteem and reaching their full potential in life. I've always tried to speak to them in such a way that would help to spark them to correct the situation that they were encountering at the time, in hopes that they would learn a valuable lesson. I would always tell them that they were not dumb or stupid, and that they could do anything they set their minds on doing with a little faith and perseverance. Whenever I would discipline them or try to correct them, I was always honest about whatever I was correcting them on, or whatever I was providing constructive criticism on in an effort to broaden their horizon.

In the beginning, I got very angry with my mother, but that anger subsided over the years and later gave me the motivation, courage, and enduring faith that I needed to understand my own daughters and turn my situation around for the better. Also, over the years, as I often thought about those hurtful words spoken by my mother, my desires to excel in life became stronger and stronger. At that point, my mother's attitude towards me back then truly became the motivating force behind all of my accomplishments; because, it was my belief that she did not expect me to excel once I became pregnant. I knew, then, I had to work extra hard to prove myself to her and overcome the type of cultural environment around me back then. Every time I thought about mother's words *"a big old mule,"* and *"you ain't gonna be nothing but have a bunch of babies and be on welfare,"* I was motivated to strive a little harder to achieve my goals and pushed further into setting continuous goals. It was something in those hurtful words about having a bunch of babies and being on welfare for the rest of my life that just didn't set well with me, and opened my eyes to reality. What my mother didn't know, or realized about me was that I truly had a will, a desire, I had the determination and the love of God, and that I was going to persevere to the end, and it was her words that put me on the right track—though she could only speak them in a way that was befitting of the situations around us. The strong-willed and determined person is who I am now, and who I was back then—nothing like the other girls in our community whom she'd thought I would model after. Finally, I was able to relate this to her that day, of my true confession at the family Thanksgiving gathering.

Parents, please listen to your children, believe in your children, respect your children; and most importantly, love and nurture your children even when they fall short of your expectations. Give them the support that they need to mature into their full potential. Don't give up on your children when the chips are down; or when things seem to be at its worse; or when they don't fulfill your expectations. Continue to lead and guide them through the good times and the bad times, because God is working it out for the good of those who love

Him. Being a parent is all part of God's big plan and we cannot change it or do a thing about it.

My mother probably assumed that with her twelve children, we didn't have to have a lot of friends because it was enough of us to keep each other entertained, busy and far away from trouble. But, even with all my sisters and brothers constantly around, it was still easy to get pregnant, much easier for a young lady to get herself into such a predicament than most people may think. However, it still does not mean that a young lady is a bad person. It also doesn't mean that she is not going to amount to nothing as a result of such a predicament. In spite of the type of situation we often get ourselves into, we can still accomplish our dreams and reach our full potential in life. We still need to be loved by our mother, family and our friends. Just pray that we all are given wisdom from God to do the right things.

Often times when we are young, our innocence takes on a whole new meaning of life—and it takes on a main role in our lives. I got myself into early parenthood, trying to please somebody—a man who was not even worth paying attention too—who was not worth pleasing in the first place, and he truly didn't deserve to change my course of life and take away my innocence. It was not so much that I was running with the wrong crowd or a bad group of people, because I went solo for the most part of my teenage years—I was not faced with much peer pressure to deal with. It was not because my mother worked two and three jobs all of my life, and was not at home most of the time. I, like a lot of other girls, made a very bad choice, of a male friend at the time, and did so without knowing the true value of self-respect, having faith in myself and in God. My mother reminded us several times that it was enough of us in our home until we didn't need additional friends, especially friends that wanted to visit and stay overnight—my mother basically didn't want to be responsible for other people children. She often told us that, "if we made our beds hard that we would have to lie in it" meaning that we would have to live with the consequences of our actions, and my first pregnancy and her words of warning came face to face with each other in many ways. I thank God for the gift of faith because faith in Him had me covered; and God also had me covered and protected by His grace and mercy that took me along the right path to this day. By having faith in God, trusting in His wings and believing that He will continue to protect me is all the assurance I needed to know that God would continue to deliver me from the snares of the fowlers and from the noisome pestilence. He will keep me covered with His feathers, and under His wings shall I continue to trust. His truth shall be thy shield and buckler.

As time passed, I came to realize that young people cannot be completely restricted from having social friends—as the ethical values and norms of society they are in, at the time, may hamper good decisions, and deter them and their parents from being open with each other on who they should or should not be friends and socialize with, and it certainly helps to prevent secret relationships. Consequently, too many restrictions and too little of the right type of communication can create problems within a family that can last for many years, or perhaps even a life time. As parents and adults, we must listen to and communicate with our children and let them know that they are loved in spite of their shortcomings as our Heavenly Father loves us unconditionally and forgives us for our shortcomings.

After I became pregnant, instead of being treated like an outcast, the black sheep of the family, or somebody my family was ashamed of—all I needed from my family at the time was a little encouragement, love and support; especially from my mother. I also needed that same love and support from all of my brothers and sisters who had already left home at the time, raising their own families. At that point in my life, just as many other young ladies, pregnant out of wed-lock, I felt all-alone and I knew then that I had to do something "extraordinary" to make a difference to make a better life for my children and me. Moreover, I felt as though my own mother did not have enough trust and faith in me to believe that I would finish school and obtain all of my other goals that I had personally set for myself. However, this was not to come true. I had to prove myself. I obtained my high school diploma, which provided me an opportunity to advance to a higher level in life than I would have, had I not graduated. Having the faith and Christ as my walking cane, I stayed focused because it was always my hearts desire to achieve my goals and dreams in life and overcome any adversities that confronted me.

I overcame that adversity, and the relationship between my mother and me turned out to be one I will always cherish deep within my heart and soul for the rest of my life. I know that I hurt her by growing up so quickly, but I spent many years trying to make it up to her by doing all of the things that I should have done before becoming pregnant. I know that I should have listened to my mother and been more obedient, finished high school, got a stable job and perhaps, started preparing for the future in a prosperous way before getting pregnant, and starting a family so soon. My mother nurtured me and raised me in a Christian home, in the manner in which God had taught her to do, and as a result of that, not only am I saved today; but, all of her children are saved and serving the Lord—she has done a wonderful job in raising all of her children. Now that I am older and wiser—Thank you mother for "a job well done." The bible says to train up a child in the way he should go, and when he is old, he will not depart from it. I know that it is to deep of an explanation for man to answer, so I asked the Lord to help me to know and understand the Love in those tears that my mother cried so deeply, so many times, for so many different reasons. Those tears she cried the day of our family Thanksgiving gathering and confession, as I spoke to her, I like to think were tears of joy, and not sorrow, that she had contributed in some way to my success.

I thank God for keeping my mother on this earth for over eighty-one years and giving me time to understand how proud she really was of me, and see how she appreciated the things I was able to do for her as a result of my perseverance. The many benefits of my hard work and determination to rise above the many obstacles, and overcome the adversities in my life have come to my mother through gifts, vacations to many exotic places such as to Hawaii, the Bahamas, Jamaica, Las Vegas, and many other excursions that are too numerous to name. Yet, the love I have for her makes what I did for her even the more sacred and wholesome; and sometimes I feel the little innocent daughter she may have felt she lost was with her all the time and never left. I've come to feel at peace with myself knowing and feeling that I was able to get back in her good grace, not because of what I'd done for her, but because like God, she never left me after all I had gone through and put her through, and was with me all the time. There is nothing in this world I wouldn't have done for my mother. All she needed to do was ask and I came through for her and she knew this to be true.

In spite of all the obstacles in my younger life, such as getting pregnant, the many adversities and the disappointments that followed, discouragements, pains and snares, I did get married, but it was not a marriage from God and resulted in a divorce approximately eleven years later. That was another adversity I had to overcome. I know that God frowns on divorces, but He still loves the divorcee. God loves us unconditionally! That marriage was very abusive and it almost stripped me of my dignity and self-esteem. I know that I should not be alive today because the last night that I was with my ex-husband, we physically fought, and normally I would not have struck him back, but that night I fought him with all the strength that I had left in my body—physically and emotionally. I felt that I was living in hell, and if I was already living in hell here on earth, I sure in the heck did not want to die and go to the one after life—but who knows, going to hell might have been a better place than where I was living—at least I thought so at the time. I was truly tired of the constant fighting and arguing until life just didn't matter anymore. Toward the end of our relationship, during the times of our conflicts and disputes, I feared not only for my life but for my daughters' lives as well, because he became more violent each day and did not particularly care who was in his path. At that point, I became very concerned for their safety and well-being. I didn't want them to grow up thinking that the way to live their lives was with an abusive man. I had made up in my mind that if the abuse happened again, I would not take it any longer. I was tired of the verbal and physical abuse. I would not take it anymore because I didn't believe that God had put me on this earth to be somebody's punching bag, or doormat to be walked all over. I wanted love and respect as a human being! I deserved and demanded love and respect—not abuse! When I decided that enough abuse was enough, and put my foot down, I didn't care if I lived or died that night; because, I was tired of the physical and mental abuse; and the constant fighting. One night he pulled a gun on me and told me, "If I can't have you, no other man will have you either." He also said that, "If I don't kill you tonight, I'll mess you up so badly that no other man will ever want you." He chased me up and down the streets and around the blocks from where we lived at the time. I ran and ran with all my strength and with all my might, because I knew, at one point, if he had caught me during the chase he would have pulled the trigger. I got tired of running, but still fearing for my life, my heart was pounding as I hid behind a tree, and when he ran pass the tree, he didn't see me. Immediately, I took off running in the opposite direction from where he was headed, still searching for me. I got back home safely and called my brother, Frank, and told him what had happened. Frank came over and managed to take the gun from the home, and the police was called. My ex-husband was arrested and was charged with assault. That night was the end of our horrible relationship. I have not looked back, nor have I thought about ever rekindling that relationship again.

If someone feels that they love you enough to want to kill you because the relationship is not going the way they think it should go—you surely don't need them. You don't need someone in your life that will literally love you to death, because if that is love—you should reconsider its true meaning. God is love! God died for us so that we could live. When the relationship becomes unbearable and a matter of life or death, they should love you enough to let you go freely in lieu of attempting to take your life or destroying you through verbal, mental and physical abuse and God will not allow it to continue. At that point, I believed that my daughters were also tired of the verbal and physical abuse and how his anger was being expressed. They began to act out their own anger by supporting me during some of the physical abuse. In other words, my whole family was being destroyed by one selfish individual and we kicked into surviving until God opened the door so that we could escape—the door to my mind, with strength and faith in Him and myself that we could make it on our own.

When you have had enough abuse in your life, and you are tired of being controlled by people that are not of God, insecure and totally out of control, you will know whether or not you want to be free from the disguise of, "I love you." Because everybody that says I love you, may have a completely different meaning of love than you.

Although the relationship with my ex-husband ended and did not work out, during the time when we were married, he was still an excellent provider. We also had some very good and enjoyable times together. The whole relationship was not a total disaster. He was just too controlling, and did not want me to grow to my full potential. He did not want me to go to college once I obtained my high school diploma; because, he had always said that he was the man of his house. Also, he would always say that he made enough money so that I did not have to work—and stated all I had to do basically was keep the house clean and meals prepared; and that I did not have a need to further my education. He even went, as far as to say that, I only wanted to pursue a degree so that I could leave him later.

After being married for about five years, and being under my husband's complete control, I decided to go to college anyway; because, I could see somewhere down the road that we would not be married, and that I would need some type of support for my three daughters and me to fall back on. But, I thank God for Jesus because if I had not listened to my heart, and the Holy Spirit, I would not have attempted to enroll in college, and I would not have anything to fall back on today. I know that God was right there through it all. When I didn't even have enough sense to acknowledge Him, He was right there! He never left my side! God said, *"I will never leave you nor forsake you. I will be with you until the end of the world."* Although I prayed while we were married, and believed that God was answering my prayers all along, somehow I was ignoring His responses; because I was to afraid too make a move. I was given all kinds of signs throughout my marriage, but I had blinders on—so I could not see what was actually lying ahead of me. I was hoping so badly that the marriage would work out, until I overlooked and blocked out a lot of the hurt and damage my ex-husband was causing to my daughters and me. However, because my ex-husband is someone's child, I often pray for him, even to this day and I truly hope that God will change his life and save his soul.

It is so very important to have an excellent relationship with God. He is so forgiving and won't let anything harm you or slip up on you if you trust and believe in Him. God said in His own word that no weapon formed against us shall prosper. I kept the faith and I kept on trusting God to bring me out of the relationship safely and unharmed. He said that He would not leave us nor forsake us, but He would be with us until the end of the world. Through prayer, keeping the faith and believing that God can and will fix the situation kept me afloat. Today, I'm free from the disguise of "I love you." Each and everyday that I live is another new day that I'm free. I thank God for setting me free—free from a bad marriage, overcoming my first teenage pregnancy, and free from many other adversities. Everyday I wake up in my right mind is a miracle. I could have been dead and sleeping in my grave but I thank God for watching over me each and everyday.

I encourage all of you to walk with God, and wait on His blessings. If you do not already have a mate, a good mate, a Christian mate—whatever you desire and need, be patient and wait on the Lord to send you a mate. Enjoy being single until He sends you your soul mate. When you feel a little lonely, take yourself out to dinner, a movie, or whatever your pleasures may be at that moment. When you feel a need to spend time with someone, treat yourself to something you enjoy, hug and cuddle yourself—you don't have to wait for someone to come along and do what you can do for yourself. Have a nice warm bubble bath by candlelight. There is absolutely nothing wrong with pampering yourself—I did it for years before God blessed me with my soul mate. It is not hard to do—you may feel awkward at first going out alone, but you will soon get accustomed to it and actually start to enjoy it as you accept your independence without fear. This is when you know that you are in good standing with God and your faith in God has been strengthened. You have reached a time of a spiritual reconciliation. Whatever you feel that you would want that mate to fulfill in your life—fulfill that need yourself just by being good to yourself until God blesses you with your mate. Also, you really do want to wait on the Lord to send you your mate because, if you don't wait on Him, you will end up with a lot of extra dead weight instead of a true mate. While waiting on a mate, you too, will have a chance to develop a relationship with God. If you just look around, you will see that so many people are single, in bad relationships, and divorced because they did not wait on the Lord for their mate.

Abstinence from sex is not the end of the world, especially as a divorcee or a teenager. If I had known then as a teenager what I know now, I would not have gotten myself in some of the predicaments that I had to deal and live with. I know now that I don't have to validate my self worth to any man.

Having self-respect and my self-worth mean far more to me now than pleasing some man's ego. Ladies, if you follow the plan that God has for your life, you don't have to be anybody's concubine or abused wife, because He will give you all the things that you desire. Though, I believe in marriage and in the union of a man and a woman as God intended for it to be—I do not believe that He intended for us (women) to be tortured and abused.

Traditionally, as human beings, we have a tendency to get involved out of desperation and get married to someone we absolutely know is not right for us in God's eyes. We as human beings, also sometimes get married out of convenience, out of loneliness, and economic gain—married for all the wrong reasons and don't wait for God to bless us. II Corinthians, Chapter 6, verse 14, calls us to purity of association. It states, "be ye not unequally yoked together with unbelievers: for what fellowship hath righteousness with unrighteousness, and what communion hath light with darkness." Having read that scripture, I believe God never intended for me to have such a mate in my life. Many of us get caught up in relationships because of sin for one reason or another; we don't pray, don't want to pray and, therefore, can't hear from God. Most of us are creatures of affection. We want affection at any cost. We have to have someone in our lives at all times—whether they are good for us or bad for us; right for us or wrong for us. But, deep down inside we know that if we wait on the Lord, that relationship will come, as God will prepare a soul mate just for you, if only you will wait patiently on Him.

While waiting for my soul mate, I went on cruises and took at least one vacation every year until I got married. This gave me an opportunity to develop a spiritual relationship with God, and I'm glad that I waited on Him.

As we grow older, we glorify in what we've come through and become, that we may help others, using our wisdom, to help guide them, and motivate them in times of their own troubles. Adversities often, though we do not welcome it, make us stronger and confident in our abilities. Adversity humbles our soul and puts us in focus with our spiritual existence.

More importantly, through adversities we learn a better way to master our failures and discouragements because we all face them in our lives in one form or another. By having faith and trusting in God can get us through our adversities. Also, we got to have patience in our souls because when we are at a point in life where we can look at everybody around us and it seems as though they are prospering and getting ahead but we are not; it may appear that they are in great relationships and we are not; they have great jobs, and we don't; and they have many more blessings than we do, we don't feel blessed. Although, it seems like they are accomplishing much more than we are; we often don't know all the struggles and pain they had to go through to get to where they are in life. We just need to wait patiently on the Lord until it is our season to be blessed.

God gives us four seasons—spring, summer, fall, and winter. In our spring years we tend to be young and innocent with great expectations for ourselves and for our parents.

In our summer years we are maturing, growing wiser and just starting to get serious about building our future both spiritually and financially. We have a tendency to struggle more with our place in life, our self-esteem, careers, relationships, and raising our children. Also, in our summer years everything seems wonderful. We are getting all of the nice things that life has to offer. It appears that we are at our highest peak and being very prosperous during our summer years. It is the summer years that God wants us to have in our lives all the time. In an effort for us to savor the warmth of summer, we need to honor the blessings and enjoy the ever-changing season of summer. If we properly prepare, the gentle happiness and joy of summer is truly ours to have and to enjoy all year round.

In our fall years, we look back upon our past and make a final determination about what we are headed for in our future, our finances, our leisure time, and start really leaning on our spiritual being. We start putting away for retirement—taking care of our children, our grandchildren, and our parents' future. While in our fall years, people should be concentrating very hard on becoming debt free and reaping the benefits of their harvest. When we are in our fall years, the so-called middle age years, we don't want nor need to be in debt. Our fall years are all about preparation. We should be sitting back, relaxing and reaping the fruit of our harvest. In our fall years, leaves began to fall, and then we start to see winter coming.

During our winter years, we have completed three seasons, and growing closer and closer to God. If we don't plan right for our winter years, when we get older, we will suffer the blows life have dealt us earlier on; because, in the winter years, it gets very cold, and it takes a whole lot more to warm us up if we haven't properly planned for this season. Our health starts deteriorating as we move closer to the end. Our faith grows stronger as we look back upon the adversities God allowed us to overcome. We even smile at the good times knowing that not everyday was a bad day. We just need to remember that God has always looked out for our best interest. He is teaching us still to trust and depend upon Him one day at a time. We need to understand that our time is not God's time but that God's time is given to us, and no matter what we are going through, He is an on-time God. When you need Him most, He will step in right on time. It appears that we cannot prosper no matter how hard we try. However, it does appear that no matter how hard we try to prosper, something else seems to get in the way. Although the seasons pass and some things go left undone, unaccomplished, incomplete—it is never too late to have a sound relationship with God as He never leaves our side. During all of our seasons, we must remember to help others that are in need—don't let Spring, Summer, Fall and Winter pass you by without lending a helping hand. Before you know it, you will be asking yourself, where have the seasons gone—who knows, you might be the next person in need of God's blessings. He has blessed you for you to bless someone else—be obedient to His word and try not to be hung up on greed.

Because of all the adversities, trials and tribulations that I encountered in my life, I could not talk about my problems with anybody for a long time, so I repressed the things in my mind, and the things in my past for years. It was very seldom that I would vent out my frustration, which was truly detrimental to my spirit. I could not grow spiritually for years because I actually hated my ex-husband for devastating my life. I actually resented being called a big old mule by my own mother. But, I went on struggling and straining to further my education, raising three daughters as a single parent, and trying to have a successful career. I was not as strong in the Lord as I am now, which was a weakness that made me somewhat co-dependent. In the beginning, I was afraid to venture out on my own. It wasn't until I had grown in Christ and was able to forgive my ex-husband for all the things that he had done to me spiritually, physically, emotionally and mentally that I was able to move on to other plateaus in my life and be completely free. Forgiving a person is not an easy row to hoe; but, we got to be able to forgive because if we don't forgive, it shows that we don't have faith in God that the problem can be fixed and that it will work—your confidence level is not working high enough, showing a very strong sign that we are weak in our faith walk.

Whenever we go through tribulations and trials of affliction it afford us the opportunity to prove what we have attained spiritually, and also help us to discover what we have not attained spiritually. We must remember that God is not the initiator of our troubles, trials and tribulations; but, when the trials, tribulations and troubles come into our life, He is willing and able to turn them around for our good. Regardless of what we are going through, He is committed to giving us the necessary strength to get through it victoriously. God uses the tribulations, trials, and adversities to form and shape His children into His likeness, the image of His Son, Jesus Christ. God uses the trials, tribulations and adversities to purge our hearts, minds and souls of distempers. He will use afflicting circumstances as sharp cutting instruments and as rough files to mold, cut and polish our soul so it can resemble God's precious Gem, the Lord Jesus Christ.

As I recall, during my first marriage, my grandmother, being very strong in the Lord, often tried extremely hard to make me see the good in my ex-husband. Also, she would try to console me by always talking with me about the problems that I was having, telling me to hang in there, don't give up and that everything would, one day, be alright. My grandmother was a praying warrior and truly believed that God was going to make a major change in me and in my situation—she was right! God changed my life! He also changed my way of thinking! She constantly told me to keep the Faith in Jesus. My grandmother was my pillar of moral support. She provided me support throughout my life and especially during those trying times. Beside God, she was definitely my source of strength. I leaned on her to carry me through most of my life's problems especially whenever I would come to a fork in the road and didn't know which way to turn. I grew to respect my grandmother's opinions and took in most of the advice that she gave so freely.

She use to always tell me that I was going to be a teacher someday—or someone very special; because, she thought I was smart enough to be anything that I wanted to be. Nevertheless, for some reason, teaching as I perceived it to mean back then just did not appeal to me; but she stayed on that teacher's kick until she went to her Heavenly home. It was as though my grandmother could foresee into the future from the wisdom of her faith that I would teach one day, not in the classrooms, but in my writing of messages and sermons inspired by

God from my own life experiences and expectations. My own trials and tribulations to help steer others along their pathways in life

After many years of dumping all of my problems on her, one day she opened up, confided in me and shared some of the things that she had gone through with my grandfather—her husband. She had been with him for about fifty years, and knew that he didn't treat her as God would have had him to do; but through it all she said, "no matter what", that she was going to stand and just believe that God was going to straighten out the problems. She said that when she married him, she made a vow to the Lord and to my grandfather that she would be with him until death; and that she was determined to keep her vows—in doing so—she did it gracefully and faithfully.

In spite of all of my pains, struggles, low self esteem, heartaches, headaches, and the list just goes on, and on, and on—I have learned to trust in God and to lean and depend upon His word, and not on my own understanding or others for that matter; because there is just no other way to survive this life's journey without Him. God is a true Friend. A true friend indeed! He is a friend because He is the One who has unquenchable Love for us all that is not diminished by our adversities. Furthermore, every time I looked around, it seemed as though trouble was all around me. I looked to my right side, and the children were causing all kinds of problems. I looked to my left side, and there too was trouble lurking me right in my face, but I kept the faith and I kept trusting and believing that one day God was going to bring me through my situations victoriously. The bible states that, *"we can do all things through Christ Jesus who strengthens us."*

Nevertheless, when all else failed, I knew that I could always count on my wonderful grandmother for moral support, encouragement, and most importantly, the spiritual guidance. Although she has gone on to her Heavenly home, yet, to this day, I still think about her daily and I still have very good memories of my grandmother. I remember mostly her laughter, her beautiful smile, her faith in God, and I admired the "elegant woman" in her. In my mind, she was the most elegant woman I have ever known, and there was no one on this side of heaven that matched her great qualities. She taught us good values and family loyalty. She taught us to believe in ourselves, to be strong, and to hold our heads high no matter what we were facing. She felt that we could do anything that we set our minds to do—and often told us so. Not only did she have the confidence in us that we could do it, she strongly believed that we could do it even better than anybody else if we set our minds to it.

My grandmother had enormous faith and confidence in her children and especially, in some of her grandchildren. She played such an important role in my life, and because of that, she lives-on in me every day. She was a great source of joy and truly an inspiration in my life. I keep her very active in me and in all aspects of my life because she was such a virtuous and wonderful person to know. I draw from her faith and strength daily. She never once displayed a selfish moment. She was always offering to help or provide guidance to anyone around her and who was in need of some spiritual direction. She was the closest thing that I had in my life to immolate or to model after, during my rearing. She was truly an inspiration to everyone she came in contact with and everybody that got to know her, just loved her persona. She had a unique voice, an expressive heart and a contagious spirit that touched hundreds of people with her inspiring and encouraging words, which on many occasions would delight your ears and inspire your imagination. So, with what my mother provided for us in her own way—my grandmother helped to reinforce it in her own way.

I truly believed that my situations would not always be as bad as they were back then, because I found that inner strength within myself from which to draw upon, especially when I was going through some of my life's struggles such as that bad marriage, raising my daughters as a single parent, holding down a job to make ends meet and later on, losing my grandmother. With the help of God's good grace, I was able to have that strength I needed to turn those challenges into tremendous motivation and opportunities.

However, I am still amazed of the perseverance and determination I had. Surprised at the strength I didn't know I had, I know that it was all a blessing from God because He said we can do all things through Him because He has strengthened us to do it. I saw a brighter future and wanted to live, for my children, for myself, and because God had given me a life that was mine to live and enjoy. Therefore, my life slowly began to change and started getting better and better, and my faith in God has grown stronger and stronger. Although I have had my share of adversities, the things that kept me from going through the lowest valleys, yet reaching the highest peaks were my faith in God, my mother and grandmother, my determination and the fact that I wanted to be able to encourage and help my family and others to overcome some of their obstacles and adversities.

I've often heard, and still hear people who are overwhelmed with the ingredients of life talk about becoming suicidal, or just killing themselves for reasons that they can no longer handle their life's situations. I have also heard how other people went all the way and other people saying that they wanted to kill themselves, but did not have the courage to go through with the suicide, and feared the pain, and the lost of their soul. Perhaps, while they were thinking about ending their lives, something (God) triggered them to think about what suicide would have done to their children, their families—and to their opportunity to eternal life in God's Heaven.

For me, suicide has never been an option. I have never thought about killing myself as a result of my trials and tribulations because God said in His words that I was fearfully and wonderfully made—and how marvelous are thy works. Why would I want to kill or destroy the work of art that God has so fearfully and marvelously made? Often I go to a very quite place where I can meditate and talk over my problems with God. Sometimes, I simply lock myself up in my bedroom and pray—but never, ever, the thought of killing myself. I much rather pray that God remove the problem out of my life and deter or change the person in my life that is causing all the trouble and grief—not end my life. I love my life too much to take it— it's a gift from God. I often thought about what would happen to my daughters if the Lord called me to my Heavenly home from natural causes, let alone me committing suicide, something that is totally unexplainable.

It is said that people who consider suicide and people who do it thinks of themselves as a means only, a thing, and not a human being. We are all human beings, and no one should take life except the one who giveth life, not even a mother or a father. We shouldn't be so selfish and want to end our lives because the stresses, and pressures of life appear to be too great for us to bear; especially when God said that He wouldn't put no more on us than we could bear. We need Jesus! Not death! If we're not saved, we're already dead in Christ. When we accept Christ as our personal Savior, we will have everlasting life.

God permits trials, troubles, and tribulations in our lives. It is through our trials, troubles and tribulations that God reveals His Power and His love for us. It is through those very problems that God uses to cause us to grow faithfully; because faith actually comes to fruition through our problems, and as a result of our trials and tribulations is when we began to realize our dependence on the Lord. God used the adversities in my life to strengthen my faith and made me much stronger, and also a more mature believer. He has taken this broken, cracked, chipped, imperfect vessel that the world had condemned, cast to the side and thought was unworthy of greatness and made something amazingly beautiful and meaningful. God often uses tragic experiences to teach us to comfort other people who must walk down the same trails and pathways that we have walked and this is what He's done for me. He also uses those experiences to turn us away from the road that leads to destruction and points us back to the pathway that leads to fellowship with Him.

God does not want us to slip into feelings of doubt and worry, because He is our ever-present help in the time of need. He gives us the constant awareness that He is our Solid Rock, our fortress, our deliverer, our refuge, our Shield, He is our strength when we are weak, and our infinite stronghold. The truth that you need to bury deep into your heart and soul is that God loves you unconditionally and He will not let you face defeat alone when you trust in Him and allow Him to direct your path. He is right there through it all. He is my Life! He is the One that stands over us night and day, and through all the situations in our lives. For every one of our challenges and trials present an opportunity for God to display His faithfulness and His love. God forgives us for all our sins. His forgiveness washes us clean and our sins disappear into the sea of forgetfulness. Whatever situation you are going through, you can stand on God's promises. He will never leave you, nor will He ever forsake you.

Maybe you, too, feel like a dusty old cracked vessel—forgotten on the shelf, or just abandoned and thrown to the side. Perhaps, you see yourself as a beautiful, shining, crystal vase, clear and unblemished. Or perhaps, you look super great from a distance and people admire you greatly from afar, but a closer look at you, reveals holes, cracks and chips from the crown of your head to the soul of your feet. You couldn't even hold a drop of water if you tried because it would eventually all leak out. Therefore, how could you encourage, uplift and inspire another human being if you are cracked and broken. Although, you may be a broken or a cracked vessel, but if you allow God to lead and guide you,

you too can be a vessel that God can use. God works through cracked vessels and chipped vessels like you and me. He will use us in astounding ways. God will mold and transform us into whole vessels that only He can use to carry out His works and good deed—not bad and evil ways, because His ways and thoughts are not like our ways and thoughts.

Instead of feeling inadequate and ineffective, and wondering why other people are being blessed by God, and used in such powerful ways to encourage and inspire others, just wait on God to perform His mighty works in your life too, and the great things He wants to accomplish through you will soon be realized. We should be praising God because He made us fearfully and wonderfully. His works are marvelous.

Thank God I was that imperfect vessel the world would never choose to use so that I could totally depend upon Him and have faith knowing that He can and would work through me to spread His goodness. I thank God for allowing me to be a broken, cracked, and chipped vessel because if the vessel hadn't been cracked or chipped, His bright light would not have been able to shine in the vessel, and I wouldn't be able to encourage others to hold-on, nor would I be able to inspire them to persevere until their change come. I wouldn't be able to share God's goodness with others because I wouldn't have the experience to share it. Although, we stumble and fall, God can still use us which shows others that we are not perfect, and that we are still targets for Satan to attack. We fall down, but we thank God that we can get up.

God is not looking for self-confident, proud people. I know that I am God's vessel, God's woman for this job—to carry forth His messages and encourage and inspire others from my own life experiences. The job to encourage and inspire others is exactly what God wants us to do. He is not interested in our many excuses that we so often come up with, nor is He interested in us wasting His time pointing out our weaknesses, because He will equip you to do the job that He calls you to do. God knows us and He knows our circumstances far better than we do ourselves, so there is no need for us to come up with excuses. God knows us completely. If we are willing to do as God directs us, He knows our capabilities and He will only ask us to do a job that He knows we can handle and achieve.

Had I been a perfect vessel, God wouldn't have had a need for me. There would be nothing I need God to fix in my life. Often, we do not know we have been fixed until after we have been broken. The bible says that, we all have sinned and fallen short of God's glory. The people who say they are perfect and who say that they are without sin are deceiving themselves and the truth is not in them. By God choosing me—this old broken, cracked and unlikely vessel, is something that the world would probably consider to have been a foolish choice, but God demonstrated through me that even His seemingly, foolish ideas and thoughts are wiser than man's wisdom could ever be. My spirit had been broken and terribly wounded, but I thank God everyday for bringing me through all of my trials and tribulations victoriously, and what I've become today validates everything that I've been through, and it has truly made every minute worth it.

Now that you see how overcoming adversities are truly done through faith in God and His Son, Jesus Christ, and understand that you don't have to be a perfect vessel for God to use you in His master plan—You will begin to gain increased confidence in God, and start walking by faith knowing that God can use you in a mighty way. He will receive all the glory, as a result of using you for the world to see His good works.

Having "God-confidence" and not "self-confidence" is trusting in God's ability to work through you to shape up people and their situations, knowing that God can get the job done. God promises to strengthen us and fight our battles if we only trust in Him. You can face any circumstance with faith, confidence and hope, because it is not your strength, your ability, your wisdom, your energy, nor your power that is the ultimate source of victory. You can tap into an eternal force that cannot be harnessed by man constraints when you place your trust in God because it is by His ability that the victory is ours, and God our Savior!

God said to count it all joy when we fall into our various trials and tribulation because it is just a test of our faith, and the testing of our faith often produces much needed patience. Whenever we have trouble in our lives we shouldn't cry as if something "terrible" has happened to us. We are to rejoice and count it all "joy"; because, God is testing us, He is testing our faith. We walk around saying that we are in the Will of God, and that we have accepted His Will for our lives, but when trouble comes, we walk around with long faces and weeping more than we are praising God, and people often wonder when they see us this way—"Where is their faith now?"

Until we can rejoice in our troubles, we are not reconciled in the Will of God. He allows troubles to come into our lives to see how we will act or react toward them. He looks at our attitudes. He looks at our hearts toward our troubles. As believers, God chastise us. There is a good purpose for our trials, suffering and testing because God said, "all things work together for a common good to them who love Him, to them who are called according to His purpose." Whenever we are placed in the fires of our adversities, troubles, tragedies and suffering, our attitude about faith should be that God has allowed these things to come into our lives for a purpose and for a season which is all part of His Master's plan which includes tests. This is all just a test of our faith. God puts our faith through these tests to prove that we are genuine.

I cried out to the Lord one day and He heard my cry. With my loud voice to the Lord, I made my request known unto Him that I needed Him in my life. I poured out all of my complaints before Him, and I declared before Him all of my troubles. My spirit was overwhelmed and weighted down with all of the problems on the earth. My enemies set snares and traps for me. It appeared to me that no one on earth loved and acknowledged me. It looked as though refuge had even failed me, and no earthly being cared for my soul. I thank God that He heard my cry. He is my refuge. He is my portion in the land of the living. He attended to my cry, when I was brought very low in life. He delivered me up from my persecutors because they were stronger than me. God brought my soul out of prison and out of bondage—out of captivity, that I might praise His holy name through these sermons and inspired messages throughout all the remaining days of my life as well as leaving my mark upon the earth after I am long gone to my Heavenly home.

I'd like to share the following poem in hopes that the readers of this novel will be blessed. When we get to the end of our ropes, and have nowhere else to turn to, consider, the "Heavens Grocery Store." It truly blesses my soul whenever I read it and reflect back over my life and see how God has been my walking cane and helped me to overcome life's adversities by bringing me through my troubles, trials and tribulations by making me a whole human being—a complete human being; and free of any disguises. Everyday that I live is a new day that I'm free in Christ Jesus. Thank God for the "Heavens Grocery Store".

"Heavens Grocery Store"
As I was walking
down life's highway many years ago
I came upon a sign that read
Heavens Grocery Store.
When I got a little closer
the doors swung open wide
And when I came to myself
I was standing inside.
I saw a host of angels.
They were standing everywhere
One handed me a basket and said
"My child shop with care."
Everything a human needed
was in that grocery store
And what you could not carry
you could come back for more.
First I got some Patience.
Love was in that same row.
Further down was Understanding,
You need that everywhere you go.
I got a box or two of Wisdom
and Faith a bag or two.
And Charity of course
I would need some of that too.
I couldn't miss the Holy Ghost
It was all over the place.
And then some Strength and Courage
to help me run this race.
My basket was getting full but
remembered I needed Grace,
And then I chose Salvation for

Salvation was for free
I tried to get enough of that to do for you and me.
Then I started to the counter
to pay my grocery bill,
For I thought I had everything
to do the Masters will.
As I went up the aisle I saw
Prayer and put that in,
For I knew
when I stepped outside I would run into sin.
Peace and Joy were plentiful,
The last things on the shelf.
Song and Praise were hanging near
so I just helped myself.
Then I said to the angel
"Now how much do I owe?"
He smiled and said 'Just take them everywhere you go."
Again I asked, Really now, How much do I owe?
"My child" he said,
"God paid your bill a long long time ago."

Author Unknown

CHAPTER FOUR

FOLDING THE NAPKIN

I have several napkins to fold, but glory be to God that one of the largest stumbling blocks in my life has been conquered and the napkin on it has been folded and tucked away forever.

I folded a napkin when I confessed to my mother that she had hurt me over twenty years earlier when she called me a "big old mule" and stated to me that, "You ain't gonna mount to nothing, or be nothing except to have a bunch of babies and be on welfare for the rest of your life!"

Stereotyping me against our environment. However, once that confession was made, my soul was comforted and I was able to move on with my life with feeling the pain from the memories of my mother's words but God eased the pain and has been blessing me over and over every since. I have prayed and I will continue to pray to God that I will never have to travel through or relive those painful pathways again. Though the pattern has been woven in that napkin and I can always open it and look at from whence I've come, just as I am sharing this pattern with my readers, I can always fold the napkin, put it away, and pray that I never have to go back to relive such a hurtful path again.

In John 20:7, it states that "And the napkin, that was about His head, not lying with the linen clothes, but wrapped together in a place by itself." Basically, what that verse is saying is that, the grave clothes were left as if Jesus had passed right through them—it appeared that He slid right out of them untouched. The headpiece was still rolled up in the shape of a head, and it was about the right distance from the wrappings that had enveloped the body of Jesus. I believe it was at this point of seeing the linen that shoaled His body that they were convinced that Jesus had risen from the dead and was no longer there. A grave robber could not possibly have made off with Jesus' body and left the linens as if they were still shaped around it. This verse may seem fairly insignificant to you. However, I personally believed, that Jesus was making a significant point when He left the tomb, stopped and made a grand gesture to declare that, that portion of His life was finished. That part of His life was over! It was history! He had risen! He was to never go back that way again—never to go back into that same situation again. That was when He folded the napkin which closed that chapter of His life, and He was never to pass that way again, and He came and He ascended to Heaven with all power in His hand. Why not do like Jesus? We, too, can walk through our past the way Jesus stepped through His grave clothes. Thou the images are still there, they are no longer a part of us and can only remain buried in its own grave, in the past, because we, too, have risen above our past. It can no longer hurt us because we are not there anymore.

Sometimes in our lives, we too need to fold some napkins after we have been clothed by them, and God has blessed us again and again to walk through them as Jesus did. Though they took on the shape of our bodies as we were inside of them, we too need to slide out of the clothing and leave the old clothes behind and start anew. Anything that keeps us from getting closer to God, we need to let it go, fold the napkin, and not pass through that way again, don't look back because it will hinder us from receiving our blessings from God.

As I write these words I am celebrating over ten years as a Christian. It states in the bible that ten is the number of new beginnings, and I do feel a real sense of renewal in my life. Being a Christian for me has been a wonderful experience. I have confessed to believe in the teachings of Jesus Christ and that He is Lord of my life. Confessing Christ is an everyday thing for me. I live it! I sleep it! I awake to it! When I think of God's goodness and all that He has done for me, I get excited! Being a believer of Christ is totally surrendering your all unto Him and allowing Him to direct all of your life's plans. He wakes me up every morning in my right mind. The alarm clock doesn't wake me in the morning. It is by God's grace and His mercy that allows us to wake up to see another day. Believe that Christ is the way to true success in the spirit, over careers, and our soul's salvation, our every awakening moments; because if you take an alarm clock to a nearby graveyard, I guarantee you that it could not ring loud enough to wake up anyone from the dead, not one soul. In all of my living, I have yet to see an alarm clock wake up the dead. I know that it is God's goodness that wakes me everyday—He is my clock that keeps on ticking. When I think about from whence I came, I can't help but to give Him the honor, the glory, and the praise. God is in total control, not man, woman, or child and I am sold totally out for Him. I have gone too far to turn around now. I have already claimed the victory over all that Satan is trying to form against me. Victory over all that he formed over me in the past. The blood of Jesus has already been pleaded and my future belongs wholeheartedly to the One who is more powerful than all creations. Growing as a Christian is a never-ending process.

As we are at the beginning of a new millennium, it is now time to fold the napkin and know that this is a time of new beginnings. Change is the key as we travel and live throughout this new millennium. I know that the most difficult thing that we do in life as a human being is the letting go of our past in order to embrace the future. We are very familiar with our past and we are just as comfortable with our past, which makes us very reluctant and unwilling to make any type of change or adjustment in our lives. We fear any type of change because of the unknown. We should seek to know the unknown, but must seek first the Kingdom of God. We should spend time being creative and positively reasonable versus negatively unreasonable and if we can think outside of our comfort zone, outside of the box we're in, we just might be surprised and return with a positive and energized spirit. If you have faith and believe in God, He will give you courage to bring about the change that you need in your life.

If we always do what we always did, we will always get what we always got. We must avoid the trap of doing things the same way just because that is how we have always done it, and because we are comfortable doing it that way.

Since change is the only thing that is constant, why not use it as an opportunity to improve or alter our circumstances. We should capitalize on every chance God gives us in life to be creative with the flow of change and grow beyond our imagination. Hard work and wisdom are just some examples for progressing and unveiling great discoveries, creations and fortunes but God, alone, is our rod and staff to lean on during our journey. We can never assume that a path that leads us one way today will arbitrarily go the same way tomorrow. We change course depending on our conditions or situations, but we should never stop moving ahead toward the Mark of the high calling. As we look to the horizon of unchartered territory, we should keep moving forward guided by the same constant compass—which is God's master plan—God's Will.

Although we may have had a very hurtful and difficult past, and it seems so much easier to hold on to it than to embrace the future, we must let go and free ourselves to pursue a brighter tomorrow. Often we fear the future because it is the unknown—the uncertainty. This is where we need to let go, fold the napkin so that we can go forward with our lives, and not pass that way again. In other words, don't look backwards because looking back hinders us from looking forward and making progress towards our future.

In order for us to use the talents that God has already blessed us with, He wants us to let go of the things that are holding us back from being elevated to the next level and being all that we can be for Him. Also, in order for God to elevate us, we must let go of all the negatively charged strongholds that are keeping us from going to the next level, and allow God to clear the path for our journey as we walk with Him, everyday and along the way.

God has His own way of changing things around for the good of those that love Him and have faith in Him, even if your faith is just the size of a little, tiny mustard seed. Thank you Jesus for that little mustard seed of faith! That girl, back then, (me) that was not going to amount to anything, but have a bunch of babies and be on welfare for the rest of her life, and the one who was most likely not to succeed has been the only child, so far, to receive a Master's Degree in her immediate family. I've never spent one day on welfare, nor did I ever receive food stamps. I simply ended up working at the Welfare and Food Stamp office for the State of Florida where my job was to issue food stamps to the less fortunate, not to receive them for myself. Thank you Jesus! I was able to start helping others, even back then, and little did I know at the time that God truly had a great plan and a purpose for my life. When I should have been dead and sleeping in my grave, or shot by a controlling husband who also tried to tear me down with words like unto those from a serpent, God saw fit for me to live so that I could offer hope to people who will listen by sharing my experiences and to encourage others who are going through the same things that I have gone through to hold on. He is not through with us yet. Oh, but when he is finished with us, we shall come forth and be pure as gold. The same is true for all of His children—when God is through with those who are not yet saved, they too will come forth with a spirit as pure as gold.

More than likely, you too have a few napkins of your own to fold. It could be old hurts, resentment, anger, a grudge, prejudice, or it could be fears of embracing change, or even embracing the future because of the way the past has gone for you. We all have napkins to fold as we face our future; but, we must face it with faith in the goodness and grace of God. He wants us to trust in Him and lean not upon our own understanding of living. He also wants us to use our talents to prosper and help others while we are here on earth.

At this point, wherever we are in our lives, we need to start anew and make a conscious decision, that we want a better life for ourselves, and let go of our current situation if they are too difficult to handle, and let God direct our path and take on our burdens so that we can rest a little while and meditate on His goodness and grace. It does not matter what type of life that we have lived; because we have all sinned and fallen short of God's glory; however, we must repent and accept Jesus Christ as our Lord and Savior, and we shall be saved. Once we are saved, we become ministers, disciples, ambassadors, teachers and evangelists—God's servants. We are now Christians; therefore, telling the unsaved how good and merciful God is and the things that He can do for them in their lives if they are only willing to be transformed into a new creature in Christ because it is only for their own good to know and act upon.

Jesus made a conscious decision. In the moment of His resurrection, when all things became new, death and the grave were conquered. In that moment of triumph Jesus stopped the significant to do what seemed insignificant, He folded a napkin—one by which our sins can all be forgiven if we come to Him just as we are.

In the moment of resurrection, as all things are becoming new in our lives, as we recognize that in Christ death and the grave were conquered, in the moment of triumph, let us stop to do the insignificant and let the act become significant in our lives. We should be sick and tired of the situations that we are in enough to know that we, ourselves, are powerless and that we want to change it. We should be tired enough at this point to want to allow God to invoke a change in our lives. So, as we have come to an end of a decade, the end of a century, and the end of a millennium, let us fold the napkin, and let us rise so that we can grow in knowing God. In our walk with Christ Jesus while getting to know Him, and in everything that we do, we need to acknowledge Him and ask God to direct our path so that we don't go down the wrong path. We must fold the napkin, rise above our past, and allow God to manifest the blessings that He has in store for us. Have a little faith and let God be your walking cane to glory.

CHAPTER FIVE
MAKING THE RIGHT CHOICE

"I call heaven and earth as witnesses today against you, that I have set before you life and death, blessings and curses; therefore choose life, that both you and your descendants may live."

We all have choices to make in our lives—some independent—some dependent—others contingent upon the Will of God. We may choose either the right way or the wrong way, and sometimes the outcome is inevitable regardless of our education, intellect or wisdom. We may choose to take all our worldly problems upon our own shoulders or we can have faith in God to carry our burdens and fix them permanently. What way will it be? God said to choose life. By the choices we make in life puts an enormous amount of responsibility upon us. "The Lord makes us strong! I heard an unknown voice that said, "Now I will relieve your shoulder of its burden; I will free your hands from their heavy tasks." He said, "You cried to me in trouble and I saved you." Psalms 81:1-7.

Believe it or not, inside all of us still exists a child who desperately needs to lean and depend on the Father—Our Heavenly Father, the almighty and all-powerful God. If you have not chosen to accept God in your life, you may not be aware that you need Him; but I am writing to convey to you and inform you that as children, regardless of our ages, we truly need our Heavenly Father's directions in our lives. Without God we are as lambs, lost in the wilderness. God tells us to trust in Him with all thine heart, and lean not unto our own understanding; but in all our ways acknowledge Him, and He shall direct our path. He has offered us directions and provided us guidance, and all we have to do is take Him up on His Word. He tells us to try Him. When God said, "I shall direct thy path", that is a promise to us from Him.

If you are feeling low in your spirit and you feel that you can't go on; just pause for a second and think, *"Did God bring me this far to leave me now?"* I don't think so! And, I do believe that God is dealing with you even at this very moment, and trying to get your attention to let you know that without Him, there is no true life—no true happiness. I also believe that God is telling you that He wants you to surrender your all unto Him, trust and believe in Him so that He can show you the Way. *You don't need to see the Way, if you just follow the One Who is the Way*; because, God is the Way, the Truth, and the Life.

For God sent not his Son into the world to condemn the world; but that the world through him might be saved (John 3:17). You are probably saying to yourself that you have lived a terribly bad life, such that you are totally ashamed of it, so much that you don't deserve any happiness and there is little or no use for you on this earth. Remember that God knows everything that you have done; and He knows just how you have lived; but He is not going to force Himself upon you. He is going to wait patiently on you to let Him in. You are probably also saying that, *"God can't possibly use a creature like me."* Don't fool yourself because you are still a child of God and a perfect prospect for God to use as one of his servants, one of His vessels, for He is a forgiving God. The only people that I know that God can't use in His plans are the ones who claim to be perfect, and the ones who feel they have nothing in their lives to straighten out or improve upon. The people who have never done anything wrong, and the ones who don't have any shortcomings—they may feel that they are already perfect—God can't use them because He hasn't brought them out of anything; thus, *they seem to think or believe He hasn't brought them out of anything,* so how would they know what God can do for them to change their situation around for the better—they can't tell others about God's goodness because they haven't been tested—they have not yet been tried in the fire. These type people would not have a testimony. They believe they have made it this far all on their own with no help from the Heavenly Father. However, you and me, on the other hand, having been broken in spirit with many, many shortcomings—we are the perfect creatures to tell the truth about how real God is, the perfect vessels for God to use in His master plan. We also have to remember that perhaps we encounter problems and situations that we cannot handle on our own or should not be in because of our disobedience to God. He states it clear in the book of Isaiah that, "The Spirit of the Lord God is upon me; because the Lord hath anointed me to preach good tidings unto the meek; he hath sent me to bind up the brokenhearted, to proclaim liberty to the captives, and the opening of the prison to them that are bound; To proclaim the acceptable year of the Lord, and the day of vengeance of our God; to comfort all that mourn; To appoint unto them that mourn in Zion, to give unto them beauty for ashes, the oil of joy for mourning, the garment of praise for the spirit of heaviness; that they might be called trees of righteousness, the planting of the Lord, that he might be glorified." If you are broken, crushed, bruised and overwhelmed with sorrows and cares, Jesus was anointed by the Spirit to heal all of your ailments.

Often we feel cursed, not realizing that it feels that way whenever we are dealing outside of God's plan for our life and doing our own thing and not allowing God to lead and guide us through our life's journey. Nonetheless, through the blood of Jesus Christ, we are saved. We are saved not only from our past; but we are also saved from the fears of failure in our present and from powerless living in our future.

Society has conditioned our minds to do and believe things contrary to God's words. If you are at the end of your rope and feel the need to make the right choice—try Jesus! I believe that you are intelligent and open-minded enough to allow me to give you a different perspective on how God sees you. Remember that you are a vessel that God can use; don't let anyone tell you otherwise because God knows your heart. He speaks to your spirit and knows what you are capable of doing far better than you do. Humans, on the other hand, look at the outer appearance, which they have no power over. Neither do they have power over heaven, nor do they have a hell to send each other too, and they surely are not in a position to judge each other; but, when each of us encounter the evils of the human mind and soul, turn to someone more powerful than any person. I am confident that once you have had a chance to allow God to work in your life, and start trusting Him more, you will want more of Him just as I did, because with Him, our lives just keeps getting better and better; and our faith grows stronger and stronger.

We also have a great inheritance that has already been promised to us by the power of God. We just hadn't physically received our bountiful inheritance yet. Having faith and trusting in God is the key to receiving our inheritance. All we need to do is claim it and work faithfully towards receiving it. You are probably also saying that you can handle all of your worldly problems all by yourself and you don't need the help of God, or anyone else, only to find out later that your problems are much bigger than you, they are greater than you could ever possibly imagine.

Furthermore, you are probably saying that you are a failure, a quitter, and that you just cannot make it on your own. This is when your problems are just right for God, and when you will know that you need to call upon the Lord for help because you have done everything that you could possibly do. Yet, if you still have a bad situation, you will continue to have a bad situation until you let go and allow God to handle it. Sometimes God will allow your plans to be deterred just so that He can show you that He is the "MAN" and He is the only one that can get us out of the situations that we so easily get ourselves into. He will allow us to experience some situations that we might not otherwise choose for ourselves. In our suffering and when we fall short of our expectations, God is never at fault. He will never fail us. We are not given a choice to pick and chose our suffering. Our suffering is not an accident nor is it a mistake. Our suffering is part of God's master plan to spiritually mature us, and it is for our good. We can choose to allow our suffering and pain to make us bitter, or we could choose to become better Christians as a result of our suffering because it is our attitudes toward our situations that God looks at when He gets ready to bless us or deliver us from our problems. Our suffering is never without God's purpose in mind. God hands are always in the trials and tribulations that we encounter in our life. He knows the plans He has for us. We always have a great blessing waiting for us once we come through our suffering. Our Christian walk comes with both pain and joy. We must learn the valuable lessons from each of our suffering experience because if we don't learn the lessons, that would be a tremendous tragedy in itself. We must deal with our problems, our sufferings head-on, because if we continue to put them off, or postpone our sufferings, that will hinder our spiritual growth and our blessings from God. Once you have given your problems to the Lord and talked them over with Him, let it go and just thank Him for being a burden bearer, and a heart regulator.

Moreover, I believe that it is necessary to encourage every thinking person to supplement Jesus Christ into his or her daily regimen. You may ask why include Jesus into your daily regimen? You should include Him because you deserve the very best and that is exactly what Jesus will give you…the very best from the bottom of your feet to the crown of your head. No other person on this side of Heaven can make that claim. *From the bottom of your feet to the crown of your head!* Your body and soul is not a trashcan. It's not a dumpster, so don't treat it as such. Also, you need to stop allowing people to dump their trash on you—their idol gossip. Just remember if you take care of your body, your body will take care of you; and if you take care of your soul, God will take care of you and save it; so don't allow the idol gossip and daily trash to land in your spirit, because if trash goes in—eventually trash will start to come out. We need to condition our minds to tune out negative thoughts and replace them with good thoughts. We can pick and choose what we want to read and hear. Perhaps, we can have daily devotion and meditate on the Word of God to get our day started. God said in His words that, "Do you not know that your body is the temple of the Holy Spirit who is in you, whom you have from God, and you are not your own?" As a Christian, I believe that God dwells within us, and that our bodies have become His home. We should try to make His surroundings as neat and clean as possible because He does not dwell in an unclean place. When we take care of our physical being and soul, we make God's temple a clean and holy place for Him to dwell in. In an effort to live for Christ, we should try to guard our ears from listening to anything that will dishonor God. Our eyes should be kept from seeing anything ungodly. With the talents and gifts from God, we should use our hands and our minds to be as creative and as innovative as we possibly can. We should make an effort to keep our tongue from speaking ill of our fellow brothers and sisters because our tongue can be as devastating and deadly as any disastrous hurricane if we are not careful in our speaking.

Besides, if you are worried about your so-called friends leaving you, not associating with you, or stop talking with you because your life has changed, don't worry about them; you just continue to ask God to decrease you and allow Him to increase in you, rise up boldly in you and pray that He will work on them also. Your true friends and family will stay around while your enemies will flee from you. God will allow your enemies to be scattered about; so you don't have to say anything, or do anything to them. Pray for them, and hope that they will eventually accept Christ, and live the life that He has planned for them to live—the same as He has done for all of us.

Also, not wanting to let go of problems is just a sign of pride and a lack of faith in God, and pride is one of those deadly sins that God hates with a passion. Often we are proud and don't want to admit that we are experiencing problems, nor do we want anyone else to know that we can not handle our own life's problems and tribulations alone; and that we do require someone more powerful than ourselves to step in to help relieve some of the burden.

Moreover, society has also conditioned our minds into believing that talking about our problems with other people is a sign of weakness—so you dare not let anyone close enough to you for fearing being called a wimp or weakling. We were created to relate to each other. God said for us to bear one another's burdens, but we cannot bear one another's burdens if we do not share the burden or talk about the burden with one another.

Did you ever stop and think about the fact that as believers we are all members of the body of Christ and each of us affects the functions of others? More importantly, just as our bodies are divided into many, many parts and subparts and each part has a very specific function which functions under the direction of our brain—we as Christians are all part of Christ's one body; we should work together under the direction, command, and authority of Jesus Christ, our Lord and Savior. Each one of us has different works to do. We have different gifts and special talents that we can all share and contribute too—that is if we all work in unity. Since we are all of one body in Christ, we all belong to each other as in one body, and each one of us does need each other.

If you've ever had a toothache, you know that your whole body feels bad all over. And think about this, a human hand severed from the body would be quite horrific, but when it's attached to an arm, the nerves and muscles are connected, it becomes extremely useful and even beautiful. What makes the difference? The difference is the relationship that it has with the body. We need the same support of each other also. That's why it's good for us to be committed to helping each other as we pray and turn to one another in either our time of need or others in their time of need. I believe as God's people we have a duty and a responsibility to uplift, inspire, and encourage each other. Christ wanted His disciples with Him during His agony in Gethesamane, and I believe it is because He wanted someone to be with Him during those agonizing moments to give Him encouragement. "For where two or three have gathered together in My name, touching and agreeing on the same thing there am I in their midst." (Matthew 18:20).

We need to depend on the Lord to carry us through all of the trials and tribulations that we encounter. We all need someone to talk to, someone to relate to, and someone to whom we can tell all the deepest secrets of our hearts to, even if we don't really want to talk about it, we need that "someone" to talk too—and help us make the right choices in life so that we won't get so wrapped up in the earthly realm and lost along the way.

So, now you see, in order for us to be complete we need to be in unity. First in unity with God, then in unity with each other as we need each other to help along the way. We need each other! We need each other's talents, intelligence, creativity, innovative thoughts, and ideas; but most of all we need to be on one accord, in unity in the spiritual life. God tells us to give our burdens to Him; He won't leave us, nor will He forsake us. He walks with us and talks with us and if we are truly listening to His voice, He constantly reminds us that we are His own, and that in itself is very comforting to us to know. When our families, co-workers and friends aren't listening—He is.

You should never feel inadequate, nor should you get angry or get an attitude when you are rejected for whatever reason because God tells us with Him, we can do all things. Instead of feeling inadequate or getting angry, we should take those obstacles and turn them into opportunities to make us stronger in the Lord. When we become angry, we should try to turn our anger into something positive. Anger causes us to act foolishly. Although, to man, it may seem like anger is the right choice for us to make, however, God said, "Do not hasten in your spirit to be angry, For anger rests in the bosom of fools." We don't want to portray ourselves as fools in the eyesight of God. We should strive everyday to become Christ-like. However, for us to become Christ-like, we must be more loving, peaceful, show more kindness toward others, be more tender and strive to be more righteous. These things are what I've come to know and live; and I pray them to be so for you, my family and friends.

We need to be very mindful that the devil and his demons work twenty-four hours a day, seven days a week, and their job is to steal, to kill, and to destroy. Every now and then, when he thinks that your mind is not on Jesus, he will try to infringe upon your weakness and convince you that you are not a child of God by whispering bad thoughts in your mind, and making you doubt your faith in God. The devil and his demons will also have you doubting your belief and your salvation; attempting to destroy your faith, your confidence, your motivation, and try to break your spirit. But, if you know for certain that you were created in the image of God, and that He died on Calvary's Cross for you, that you may have everlasting life—then nothing, nobody or anything, for that matter, should be able to change your belief or shake your faith when you are anchored in the Lord. If you become weak and allow Satan's evil thoughts to creep in, you will always feel inadequate, defeated and you will always feel that you are not worthy to work for the Lord. You will probably feel that way until you truly accept God into your life, which paves the way for you to enter into the Kingdom of God. He is the way, the truth and the life—without God there is no life, and He alone is your answer to overcoming evil by making the right choice to allow Him to be Captain of your ship.

Meanwhile, once we have entered God's Kingdom, He wants us to have a personal relationship with Him, and the only way that we can have a personal relationship with Him is to read our bible in an effort to get to know Him better and just communicate with God on a daily basis. Praying and singing praises to His holy name until you can feel His anointing fall down on you; because, we must worship God in Spirit and in Truth. This is all part of being born again and it also signifies that you're growing in faith. Once you have accepted God, you can speak boldly with confidence. You won't need anyone to tell you that you are inadequate because you know, that you know, that you are a child of the Most High. You are living the way that the Lord has chosen for your life. God sits high and looks low, and in Him, there is no big I's and little You's; we are all equal in His eyesight. He has no respect of person. However, God sanctify and will set His children apart from the worldly children. Once we accept Christ as our Savior, we are forgiven of all our sins and then we are set apart for His usage and His glory. However, complete sanctification begins when we die, and it is completed when our spirits are reunited with God resurrected body. God will continue to work on our shortcomings until He perfects us and call us to our Heavenly home. He will teach us to be patient and wait on Him—patient with our children, our families, ourselves and with Him. Once we've completely accepted Him, He will show us clear understanding of the young, the old and the evil ones. We will come to accept the imperfections in our life and He will steer us around them, and help us to overcome them by trusting in Him to be the heart fixer and the mind regulator. When we get aligned with God's purpose and plan for our life, we will be blessed, and no good things will He withhold from them who walk in righteousness.

Friends, I summit to you that God makes no mistakes. He is able to take your life with all of your shortcomings, all of the heartaches, all of your pains and sufferings, all of the disappointments that you have encountered over the years, all of the regrets and all of the missed opportunities that you may have had or think you have had in your life, and still use you for His glory. When you have a trial in your life use it to rise higher. You cannot become champions without a fight. You cannot claim victory if you don't allow God to help win your battles. He is in charge of your life and of the entire universe and the destiny of every living soul thereof lies in the palm of His hand. Remember that God made you a promise that *"Joy comes in the morning."* I believe that the sun is already starting to rise in your life, because, if you are reading this book— that's a blessing—that is a bright spot in your life. It is a sign that you are seeking to make the right choice. I know that God has spared your life and allowed you to see another day that you have never seen before, and a day that you will never see again. A day that you can rediscover Him and step up and take your stand to be who God wants you to be and who you should be—to be a responsible child of God in a way that you will surrender to your own peace, confidence, self-respect for yourselves and others—and most of all, opening the door of your heart to let God in once and for all.

If you have already had many trials and tribulation in your life, then, God has inspired me to tell you that your future will be better and brighter than your past, and you are certainly blessed just to be alive and in your right mind. However, the only thing He states that you need to do is develop a realistic plan of action to attain the life that you deserve and the life that God has already planned for you—by allowing God's plan to work for you. God is only thinking of our best interests. He always has our best interest at heart. What a mighty God we serve! You will soon feel so good inside because you just know that everything is going to be all right. God has rebuilt many cities and repaired many broken hearts and souls. He will not sit idly by, silent and inactive when we pray to Him for help. He will destroy the very memory of the days when our enemies tried to destroy us and blow them away like dust. So, while you are trying to make the right choices in life, picking and choosing what to do and what not to do, allow me to offer you some suggestions to incorporate into your daily regimen so that you may be more fruitful in your life. These following choices can only enhance our relationship with Jesus Christ. The suggested choices are stated so eloquently in the following poem. My only hope is that you make the right choice when planting your own personal garden because you reap what you sow. It's now time to plant your garden. As you began to plant your garden, allow me to suggest the following "VEGETABLES":

PLANT three rows of squash
Squash gossip
Squash criticism
Squash indifference

PLANT three rows of peas
Purity
Patience
Perseverance

PLANT six rows of lettuce
Let us be unselfish and loyal
Let us be faithful to duty
Let us search the scriptures
Let us not be weary in well-doing
Let us be obedient in all things
Let us Love one another

NO GARDEN is complete without turnips.
Turn up for church, prayer service, and Bible study.
Turn up with a smile, even when things are difficult.
Turn up with determination to do your best for God's cause.

Author Unknown

After planting your garden, and making the right choices, may you "Grow in Grace and in the knowledge of our Lord and Savior Jesus Christ." II Peter 3:18

CHAPTER SIX

ENCOUNTER WITH THE ANGELS

"And it shall come to pass in the last days, saith God, I will pour out of my Spirit upon all flesh: And your sons and your daughters shall prophesy, and your young men shall see visions, and your old men shall dream dreams." (Acts 2:17).

Angels are God's messengers. They are spirit beings, created by God. They were created to be servants of God, to perform the Will of God in the earth. They are of various colors, ranks, abilities, and have many different duties. Angels are personal beings who represent God. I believe that they have influenced, either directly or indirectly, over the lives of everyone on earth. They appear in every culture and have played a major role in almost every religion and are far more active in human affairs than most people would ever suspect or imagine. Angels are God's secret agents, and you will know it, and recognize them when they come into your presence, or personally speak to you. Spiritual help is always available from the angels. They are caretakers of our souls and their love is everywhere. They may appear in dreams as visible as normal human being; or they may appear as beings of brightness with a glow about them, in a light, or in shinning garments. They are incredibly powerful, and have great intelligence and wisdom. Angels are greater in power and mightier than we are. They are responsible only to God and are under His direct order to do His will. Angels are God's Heavenly hosts. They often come in times of death to escort us on over to the other side, or difficult times when we are tired and weary, or just during normal encounters to remind us that God is real.

By putting God first, and trusting Him as our redeemer He promised that the outpouring of His spirit will be upon all ages, types and classes of people. The outpouring of His spirit will bring full deliverance and salvation.

Late 1994, the Holy Spirit woke me up out of a deep sleep about two or three A.M. to bring me good tidings. That morning was a morning that I will never forget; because, that is when the angels came to me in a semi-dream state, and told me that God had blessed me with my husband, and that his name was "Mr. Jackson." It seemed as though I was awake, but I suppose I was partially asleep, partially dreaming, and while in this state—caught between the two worlds—real and spiritual—while lying on my back gazing towards heaven and around my bedroom trying to collect myself—there appeared on both sides of the bed two angels, clothed in white linen with a bright, almost blinding glow about their bodies. I could not see their faces as the light around them made it so very unclear—it was just too blurred—but I could see the outline of their bodies. As I gazed toward the angels' faces, the one angel to my right spoke and said in a soft voice, "Your husband is Mr. Jackson." At first, I was somewhat frightened and skeptical; but the experience was so awesome, so overwhelming—it was a revelation. Of course, when that revelation came to me, I had all kinds of questions and reservations as to "why him" because he was not my type—at least that is what I initially thought. What I had envisioned or expected for a husband was a businessman, dressed in a three-piece suit, financially stabled, outgoing, and spiritually sound. I had been asking God for a man who first loved Him, and that he might know how to love me and treat me with respect if he knew how to first love God.

This encounter with the angels was one of the most unique but marvelous experience I had ever had—an unforgettable encounter because it was as though I was in a place of comfort—Heaven! We hear and talk about heaven, but that morning I actually felt as though I was in heaven in the presence of God's-loving angels. I couldn't imagine a place so beautiful—it was truly like heaven—it was such a beautiful image. It was the perfect place to "chill out" and talk with the angels. Again, I wanted to know why him; and the Holy Spirit answered through the angels, "Why not him, you asked for someone who loved the Lord?"

And I replied, "Because he is not my type."

So, as I laid there thinking about what had just happened, I went back and forth challenging the angels in hopes that it may have been a mistake. Then, I thought, after realizing what I had asked God for, it couldn't possibly have been a mistake because God does not make mistakes.

The Holy Spirit said that Mr. Jackson will be my head. Having been divorced and single for sixteen years and being a strong-willed woman, I had major problems accepting the fact that he was going to be my head because I was totally independent. The angels would not leave until I accepted my blessings. So again, I challenged the angels and said, "what do you mean my head"?

And the Holy Spirit said, "Just as I'm the head of the Church, man is the head of his Wife."

I had a real problem with that at first until I got out of bed—still in a dream state, but it was so real, and read 1 Corinthians 11:3 where God said "But I would have you know, that the head of *every* man is Christ; and the head of the woman is the *man*; and the head of Christ is *God*."

At that point, the angels and I were still wrestling, and once I had finished reading that verse, I reached up toward Heaven with both hands, and pulled down my blessings and I started thanking God for my husband. It was at that moment that I fell in love with him, (my husband) because God said He had blessed me with him and that settled the debate between the angels and me.

I guess one could say that when the two angels came to bring me the good tidings, it seemed as though I was being so ungrateful; because I didn't accept my blessings right away. However, it wasn't that I was being ungrateful, though—but I thought to myself, surely God could do better than that for me—after all, I had been waiting patiently for three years for Him to bless me with my significant other—my soul mate, and the ideal husband that He had designed for me.

It is a gift and very comforting in believing that you truly have an angel—a guardian angel. I have had many angels in my life. I have had financial angels. As my dinner guest while I was single, I had a place setting at my table for my angel who I believe joined me quite often because I use to smell the fragrance when they passed by me. Also, the Lord has put in my path and surrounded me with a guardian angel to protect me from all harm.

When I met my husband, he was teaching trainable mentally retarded students which meant that he could not dress as a businessman, nor could he dress like a regular pubic schoolteacher. Some of the children he taught had serious medical problems such as seizures and other medical problems that he had to assist with during their episodes that prevented him from dressing business-like.

Although, it was three years later, from 1994 to 1997, before Lacey (now my husband) and I got married, I still thanked God everyday for him because it was so plain when the angels appeared to me in that dream, and delivered the awesome message to me that Lacey was the one. During those same three years, other men came into my life and we attempted to date. We would go to lunch or dinner and that would be the end of the relationship because it was clear that they just weren't the men that the Lord had picked for me. However, the man that the Lord had blessed me with, did not show any interest, and there was no courtship, nor engagement. Time passed and I remained single and uncommitted. Then, it "just happened." Seven months before we got married, he finally called and asked me if he could take me out to dinner for my birthday—this caught me totally off guard. I was so surprised by the fact that he called to ask me out to dinner, and before I knew it or realized what I had said, I told him "yes."

Lacey and I had dinner on 13 February 1997, and that was our first so-called date. My youngest daughter graduated from the high school where Lacey was teaching, and I believe she told him when my birthday was while she was still attending, he never forgot it, and used it when it was convenient for him to make his move to ask me out. Also, about the same time that I had the encounter with the angels in a dream, Lacey had told a Deacon at the church where we both were attending that, "one day I was going to be his wife." After we started making wedding plans, he told me that he and the Deacon were riding in the same car, on the same street as the high school where he worked, and was teaching school, and as they passed me that day driving my car, he pointed at me and said, "I'm going to marry her."

Lacey, in his special way, and with his unique personality, not looking directly at me, with his face turned slightly straight in front of him, indirectly proposed to me, May 1997, over Mother's day weekend.

It was one bright and sunny afternoon as Lacey and I were together riding down Interstate 65 through Montgomery, Alabama, with the car windows slightly cracked as a nice cool breeze from the fresh air blowing in. He'd come straight to the point and said, "I've got to buy a ring."

"What"? I replied.

He repeated, "I've got to buy a ring."

"For what?" I replied.

He quickly answered, "So you can wear it!"

"Don't you have to ask me something first?" I asked.

He said, "No, we're just going to do it."

"Do what?" I replied.

He laughed and never said exactly what it was that we were "just going to do." At that point, I began smiling with my face turned slightly toward the passenger's window, where I appeared to be gazing out of the window and my mind started wandering if he could possibly have meant marriage.

A few minutes later into the conversation, he said, "The only time that I will be available to _'do it'_ will be the third weekend of November 1997," and that was when I knew exactly what he was talking about.

I said to him, "No way!"

That was the same weekend that I had gotten married to my first husband, and that date was totally out of the question. Not that I believed in omens. I just didn't want to associate my blessing from God with the mess that the devil and I had previously made.

He then stated, "the only other date available for me is the second weekend of September, 1997", and that is when we _"did it."_ Bless the Lord.

God is so good and so true to His word. We got married, and to this day, Lacey never directly asked me to marry him. We just _"did it."_ There was nothing traditional about our relationship or marriage for that matter, and it was just the way it was prophesied to me. A few months after the encounter with the angels, I began preparing the wedding ceremony program, which was approximately two and a half years prior to us getting married. I basically prepared it sitting in church service one Sunday morning while the service was going on.

The angels that the Lord allowed to appear before me in that dream was the best _encounter of any kind_ that I have ever had in my entire life, and it came to pass. Lacey is now a true reality in my life. God said in His words that, " I will pour out of my Spirit upon all flesh; and your sons and your daughters shall prophesy, and your young men shall see visions, and your old men shall dream dreams." Today, I am living that prophesy from the angels.

Since Faith is the things hoped for, and because I kept hoping—God blessed me and I'm living the evidence of the things that I could not see. Faith shows us how to look forward to things hoped for; and all we need to do is to have faith and wait patiently on the Lord to make good on His promises.

If God has ever told you that he was going to bless you with something, stay faithful, and trust Him to bring it to pass; because, if God says it, He will do it. I am truly a living witness of that testimony that if God says that He is going to bless you, He will do it if you wait patiently on Him. He does not need us to help Him do His job. If God put a dream in your spirit or send you a prophecy, don't let anyone or any situation rob you of such a blessing. Don't let doubt, disappointments, loneliness, the devil, people, discouragements or any other obstacles prevent you from carrying out your dreams; because if you can conceive it in your spirit, you can definitely achieve it through Christ Jesus.

Perhaps, you too can call upon your guardian angel to help you through your difficult times, your peaks and valleys as I have. Angels are real. The question is—Will you recognize your angel when it appears, or will you ignore it? When you come in contact with your angel, your life will be changed forever— the encounter with your angel will truly be life changing and very personal. I would like to share with you an inspirational angel poem a friend sent to me. It is just a little something to ponder over about guardian angels; perhaps, to even help you recognize your own guardian angel. Enjoy!

I'm your Guardian Angel.
I am a tiny angel
I'm smaller than your thumb,
I live in peoples pocket,
That's where I have my fun.
I don't suppose you've seen me,
I'm too tiny to detect,
Though I'm with you all the time,
I doubt we've ever met.
Before I was an Angel...
I was a fairy in a flower,
God, Himself, handpicked me,
And gave me Angel power.
Now God has many Angels
that He trains in Angel pools,
We become His eyes, and ears, and hands
We become His special tools.
And because God is so busy,
With way too much to do,
He said that my assignment
Is to keep close watch on you.
When He tucked me in your pocket
He blessed you with Angel care
Then told me to never leave you,
And I vowed always to be there.
I'm your Guardian Angel.

Author Unknown

CHAPTER SEVEN
COUNTING MY BLESSINGS

For years, I had been praying and asking God for three specific blessings among several other blessings; a husband; to save my children; and to bless me to leave Montgomery, Alabama and enter into another career. As a result, January 1997, everywhere I went, everywhere I looked, it appeared that the Holy Spirit was always speaking directly to me; telling me that this was my year—my year of *Jubilee*. When I turned on the television, even the ministers would be pointing their fingers in the direction of the screen as though they were speaking directly to me, and saying, *"this is your year."* So finally, I started thanking God for those blessings that I had been asking Him for; because, I believed those were signs confirming the blessings that the Lord had already whispered into my spirit, especially during my encounter with the angels three years earlier in 1994. Also, all the way through March 22, 1997, I was still hearing that this was my year. On that day as I was attending a crusade in Atlanta, GA where a Bishop was speaking—it was that day when all of my blessings were again confirmed.

God used the Bishop through the Holy Spirit to bring forth the final confirmation that this was truly my year of jubilee to receive some of my heart's desires. The Bishop from the pulpit conveyed the confirmation for my three specific blessings one Saturday afternoon just as I had been asking God and describing the blessings for years. I could not believe it! It was another true prophecy. He said, "that husband" whom I had been asking God for, that God was going to bless me this year (1997). Those "children" whom I had been praying for salvation for, would be saved.

Finally, the Bishop said, "Pack your bags, put them by the door and wait; because you will be moving and you will be promoted." He also said that, "God is going to bless you with a job that is going to blow your mind." It was going to blow my mind because I wouldn't have the experience to fully qualify. I had never done the type of work before, which the job called for. He stated that others would be more qualified to do the work but that job would be "just for me." I was so overwhelmed with joy and amazed by the confirmation of my three specific blessings from the Bishop, and believed that he was truly speaking from

God who'd been listening to all my prayers. I was astonished—moved deeper into my faith, which by now was no longer the size of a mustard seed; but, maturing into a full-blown relationship with God. Although my blessings were confirmed, I knew that eventually I would be receiving them because God said they were mind. However, I had to remain firm in my faith to receive them. Sometimes, we may not be quite ready to handle the blessings that the Lord has in store for us to receive. God may put your blessings right in front of your face, almost, close enough for you to reach out and touch them, or taste them, but you must have faith in God because if not, He backs up, maybe one year, two years; perhaps, even ten or twenty years before He actually gives the blessings to you just to ensure that you are faithful to Him and ready to receive the blessings that He has planned for your life.

I still thanked God everyday for my blessings that I had not yet received. Never once did I get discouraged, nor did I believe I wouldn't get my blessings.

On one very hot, gorgeous and sunny Saturday afternoon, in the fall, in Montgomery, Alabama, on 13 September 1997, God allowed Lacey and me to reach that decision and we got married. He allowed us to have a sacred wedding ceremony and to unite our lives as one with Him, and to place our love and future in His hands. We had a fairly large church wedding with forty-eight wedding participants and over two hundred guests attended. The wedding was so beautiful! The colors were purple, gold and ivory. It was not the traditional wedding that you would expect to attend. We invited our guests to *worship* with us and to witness our vows. The fifteen bridesmaids were so beautifully dressed in purple—the color of royalty. The matron and maid of honors were dressed in gold—the other color of royalty just as gorgeous as they wanted to be. The soloists sung from their hearts many beautiful songs, "Jesus is the Center of My Joy," "Flesh of my Flesh," "Jesus is Love," "Saints Hold On," "We Come This Far By Faith," "You Know," "Everything is Gonna Be All Right,"—and many more—it's just too numerous to name. Then, I walked down the aisle not on "Here Comes the Bride," but I walked down the aisle on, "Order My Steps," which was truly a blessing, because God had brought us together and was guiding my steps towards the altar.

Another blessing was when my three children started going to church. Two of my daughters have since given their life to Christ, and I can count this blessing also.

The blessings kept on coming. While assigned to Gunter Air Force Base, in Montgomery, Alabama, on 18 December 1997, I was on a temporary duty assignment in Biloxi, Mississippi, when I was tracked down for an interview for a position at Wright-Patterson Air Force Base, in Dayton, Ohio, which was a higher-level position than I was currently assigned to. The interview process began. There were three high-ranking managers that interviewed me. I answered all of their questions to the best of my ability. However, I was just going through the routine, the formality of the interview and I didn't think that I had much of a chance because I am not a technical person. I didn't think that I had done such a good job on the interview; as most of the questions were very technical in nature and my background is in management and acquisition logistics. However, I reflected back on the day of the crusade that I had gone to in March 1997 where the Bishop had predicted that I wouldn't be fully qualified for the new job but it would be designed just for me because no one else had filled that position before. Again, God came through for me and I got the job. God said, *"When praises go up, blessings will come down."* I stayed prayerful and I kept praising God through all of those months, until all of my blessings had been manifested.

God should be praised for His greatness, because He is worthy to be praised. Praising God is your best weapon against the devil. When we praise God, it produces victory, and in return, victory evokes praises. We bring God glory when we praise Him.

When the confirmation of my new job came, tears just started rolling down my face. I was so overjoyed with gladness because there were only seven days left in the year and God had already told me that this was my year of jubilee, and my blessings had already been confirmed and I was just waiting patiently for all of them to materialize. God will not lie to us. If he promises He will do something for us—He will do it. I shall never forget that day. It was 24 December 1997, at exactly 09:58 A.M., (seven days before the end of the year) when the phone call came. The selecting supervisor for the new job was on the other end of the phone, from Wright-Patterson Air Force Base, Ohio.

She asked me, "How would you like to move to Dayton, Ohio?"

I was very shocked, but I was not surprised; because, God had already told me back in March of 1997 through the Bishop to pack my bags, put them by the door and wait because I would be leaving. So I asked the supervisor "When?"

She replied, "How soon can you get here?"

I answered, "How about 15 February 1998?"

She stated, "I need you sooner, how about 01 February 1998?"

Accepting 15 February 1998 would have given me between 45-60 days to pack up and move from Montgomery, Alabama, to Dayton, Ohio. So, I hesitated and thought to myself "Well", *since I'm a praying warrior, perhaps the career's program in which I am registered in and was selected from, its procedures and guidelines probably wouldn't allow the paperwork to get processed by 01 February 1998.* So, we decided to let the Career's Program process determine how soon I would report to my new workstation.

Just as I'd thought, personnel and management couldn't get the paperwork processed in time for me to start 01 February 1998. Thus, my effective date to be assigned to Wright-Patterson AFB was set for 15 February 1998. Praise God, because I had too many things to do in preparation for the move in such a short period of time. Again, that just goes to show us what God has planned for us, no one can stop it, and it shows us that God is on our side, and He wants only the best for His children. This blessing showed me these things and I am still enjoying this blessing and promotion that God has given me. God is truly an "on time God." An awesome God!

Again, this too helped me to count all of my blessings and start giving God all the thanks, all the praises, and all the glory for being so good and so faithful to me.

Getting the new job and the opportunity to start a fresh career that took me up from the south and farther away from the environment of my past was the last one of the three blessings that I had asked God for and had gotten confirmation on through the angels and the Bishop. Once the last blessing had materialized and I moved to Dayton, Ohio where I began working at Wright-Patterson Air Force Base, I continued to cry and praise Him because He is so good and so true to His word. If God says it, that settles it.

Through all of those confirmations and dreams, wishing, hoping, and praying, I kept the faith. I kept believing that God was going to come through for me.

In the book of Isaiah, God says in His own words—"They that wait upon the Lord shall renew their strength; they shall mount up with wings as eagles; they shall run, and not be weary; and they shall walk, and not faint." (Is 40:31). For the first time in my Christian walk with God, I truly understand and believe the words in that verse. By waiting patiently on the Lord, my faith has truly been strengthened. My belief and trust in God have gotten much stronger. My faith was tested many times to see if I could endure the wait until my blessings were manifested—and I did.

God will also challenge us to go beyond our abilities. He will give us a blessing that will absolutely blow our minds. He will also give us blessings, which he knows that we know would be too great for us to have, or handle, or for us to ever imagine or comprehend. He said in His words that ears hadn't heard, nor eyes seen all the blessings that He has in store for us. Many, many great things and we must groom our hearts, minds, bodies and souls to recognize them when they come to us and count them by giving Him all the honor and praise that He greatly deserves.

Don't be afraid of your weaknesses; because, God will equip you to do whatever He calls or tasks you to do. Just have enough faith in Him to receive His blessings unconditionally. When He blesses you, whether it is something you have been praying for a long time to happen, or something new, thank and praise Him for the blessings when they come, and are manifested in your life, share them with others that they, too, may become true believers.

Moreover, when I think about all of my many blessings as compared to my triumphs and tribulations, I don't just think about all of the material blessings that make me happy, but, I also think about something far more important—the simple things in life that we so often forget and take for granted—things such as how much happiness and joy that my family and friends bring into my life. Also, I think about my health, my strength, and my ability to help others—all of which bring me peace and closer to God. It is these simple things in life that's all around us, but often we seem to take them for granted and forget to count them as blessings but they produce the most peace, joy, and happiness in our lives. So, you see that God has been too good to me which is why I give Him the praise by spreading His goodness—His Word. I am truly too blessed to be stressed, or to be worried about worldly things.

My Bible tells me to lean not unto my own understanding but in all my ways acknowledge Him and He will direct my path. Through it all, I have learned to trust God and I have learned to depend upon His Word. By "counting my blessings" everyday and all along the way, is truly how I have overcome things brought upon me in the world so far and I have shown and will continue to show that I know God is my rod and my staff. He's been my shelter in a mighty storm and always with me, around me, and guiding me in all that I do. God's Grace and mercy is sufficient to carry me through whatever I must face. It is Grace and faith that we need to have in order to go through this life's journey. It was God's Grace and mercy that saved Daniels from the Lion's Den. It was His Grace and mercy that saved Shadrach, Meshach and Abednego from the fiery furnace. It was God's Grace and mercy that allowed the children of Israel to cross the red sea without drowning, nor did any harm come to them. GRACE was put on the cross at Calvary so that we don't have to endure the pain He did. We should continuously count our blessings because Jesus Christ suffered so we didn't have too. It was God's Grace and Mercy that brought me through. Why not let His Grace and Mercy bring you through too.

CHAPTER EIGHT

TRIUMPHS OVER TRIBULATIONS

God said, "For whatsoever is born of God overcometh the world: and this is the victory that overcometh the world, even our faith. Who is he that overcometh the world, but he that believeth that Jesus is the Son of God?" When God speaks of whatsoever, He is referring to every believer born of God; and there is victorious power through this confession because God is sovereign over the world, and only through the Son does man have access to and find favor with God and in God.

Imagine having a child that you love so much, you love that child with all of your heart, with all of your might, with all of your being and soul telling you that they hate you and calling you names that you dare not repeat. Imagine having to have your child declared as an adult at the age of seventeen because they were totally out of control. Also, imagine your relationship with that child deteriorating to the point that it would be in the best interest of the other family members for the troubled child to live outside the family home.

By the time my daughters reached their teenage years, my ex-husband had been gone for a few years, and basically, did not play a major role in their upbringing. My daughters went through the terrible teen years for approximately three years during which time they were constantly disobeying the family rules—the rules of our home. The two oldest daughters' behavior became unbearable until it was almost impossible for us to live in the same house without disagreements on a constant basis. They would jump out of their bedroom window; or when they left the house for school; or whatever they may have left home for—they didn't return home for long periods of times. To me, that was very painful because I feared that they weren't up to anything good when they would do that. Sometimes, I even felt harm was going to come to them. It happened so often that once I got their behavior patterns down to a science, and knew about when they would make their next move to escape—routinely, I would lay in bed and anticipate them escaping, but I could not do a thing but call on the Lord. Many nights I laid awake in bed praying that my daughters would not try to escape through their bedroom window, and do the right thing by trying to be obedient. Also, I wanted them to enjoy their childhood years without growing up so quickly, as I did. A good mother never wants her children to grow up too fast, which I suppose was the message my mother was conveying to me in her own way—and it's difficult for a young teenager to absorb the impact of their inappropriate behavior prior to going through the consequences themselves as derived from their own experiences.

Many nights when my daughters jumped out of their bedroom window, I could hear their feet when they met the ground; my heart and soul ached for their lack of wisdom. Initially, for the first few times, I would call the police and inform them of the problem that I was experiencing with my daughters. The police would find them and bring them back home, or at least talk with them about peer pressure, their behavior, and disobedience. Then, the problem got too big for me to handle, to the point that I had to take it to a higher power, the Lord in Prayer, and turn it over to Him. Once I turned it over to the Lord, after they escaped out of their bedroom window, I would simply get up, go into their bedroom, pull the window back down, lock it and return to my bed where I would eventually fall asleep.

Finally, one of my daughters and I went to visit a lawyer to seek legal advice on how to declare her as an adult. Once we got to our appointment, the lawyer prophesied to me. She told me that, "one day everything was going to be all right, because I was a good mother, and that I just had a troubled child who was only trying to find her way in life and fit in with her peers." She prayed for me and for my daughter while we were in her office, and she told me that God had something special for me to do. He had a plan for my life. She stated, while holding my hand in prayer that it was a sensation, a feeling that had come over her and at that moment she was able to tell me that everything was going to be all right. She stated that same child who was causing me all the grief, all the heartaches, and all the pain was going to make me proud one day. She told me that all of the problems would eventually come to pass and be put behind us. After that powerful prayer, and once we were able to collect our bearings and thoughts, she told me where I could go to obtain not only free counseling for the problems that we were having; but also assistance in declaring her as an adult.

I was a single mother trying to raise three daughters alone with barely any support financially, emotionally, or physically from their biological father; and at the same time trying to go to college to obtain my Bachelors degree.

It's so good to know that God has His angels positioned everywhere. I say this because that lawyer was truly God sent and I really, really needed to hear from heaven, and I needed to hear those very kind words that day, because I was at the end of my ropes with the persistent problems with my child and it was causing me to feel so low in my spirit—even on that particular day. There were times when the pain got so severe—so unbearable, that I wanted to walk away from it all. I thought about unconditional love and how I needed to just stand and wait on the Lord to fix things for us. I had never experienced going into a lawyer's office where the session was stopped in mid-stream so that a prayer could be conducted with me and for me. Nor had I ever experienced being told during such a prayer that I was very special and that God was going to use me one day. I liked the sound of, "God using me someday," and hearing that comment from her had a nice ring to it. I didn't quite understand it at the time, but it stayed with me for over ten years and now I can finally see what she meant.

Although, my second oldest daughter and I had to go through mediation and get a legal memorandum of understanding and had an agreement drawn up for the purpose of reducing the conflicts that had developed over the years in our relationship, I continued to have faith that God would see us through it. We acknowledged that our relationship had deteriorated as she grew up, and that we could no longer live together under the same roof as a family. However, I truly believed that going through all of those pains, trials and tribulations were all part of God's plan for our lives. It was a process in which we had to go through for God to bless us, elevate us, and bond our family in order for us to have a sound relationship—that wholeness that He wanted it to be. God wanted us to first be humble and serve Him; then, He wanted us to rise up above the miscommunications, misunderstandings, and stubbornness in order to appreciate who we really were—a family that should having been bonding and holding together instead of coming apart, especially in times of crises.

Today, thank God, the relationship with my daughters has rekindled. We reached a bond and have shared so much throughout the years—the triumphs and the joys; the disappointments and the tears. Today, we share our fondest memories, hopes and dreams; we share and enjoy good times together. We share a special kind of bond that we know will last until eternity. We also know, without a shadow of a doubt, that we share a special kind of closeness that has developed through the years and no one can ever change that because through much prayer and supplication, God has bonded our relationship back together as it should have always been. We have a great relationship and with the Grace of God, it will continue to keep getting better and stronger. On the other hand, if it had not been for God on my side, I don't even want to know where I would be today. I could have lost my mind, but Glory be to God, He kept me sane through it all. He was right there all the time—all the way—every hour of the day. Thank you Jesus! Victory is mine!

Another triumph over a tribulation that I had to overcome was being extremely fearful and very nervous about speaking in front of a group of people. I had a powerful story and testimony to tell; however, I could not tell it without getting very emotional because of the fear and the anxiety that came with it. Therefore, the only way that I knew how to overcome and conquer the fear of speaking in public was to confront it head-on. So, several years ago, I decided to join an organization entitled, "Toastmasters International" to learn how to overcome that fear.

Toastmasters International is an organization that is the leading movement devoted to making effective oral communication a worldwide reality. It helps people learn the arts of speaking, listening, and thinking—vital skills that promote self-actualization, enhance leadership potential, foster human understanding, and contribute to the betterment of mankind. The Toastmasters program allows one to develop skills, which lead its members toward becoming the self-assured, successful person that they want to be. It provides them the ability to organize their thoughts and present those thoughts clearly and confidently, listen critically, and lead others.

I also had another very special reason for wanting to learn public speaking, a reason that grew out of the fact that I prayed and asked God to reveal a purpose for my life. I was later to learn and truly believed that my purpose in life is to inspire, encourage and minister to others.

I have made enormous progress towards overcoming the fear of speaking before an audience and I will continue to conquer the fear because I know that God did not give me the spirit of fear; but He did give me the spirit of love, power, and a sound mind. I will use this power, spirit of love, and a sound mind that God has given me to bring this obstacle of fear to realization and eliminate it so that I can continue to fulfill my purpose in life, and I encourage others to do the same. FEAR is nothing more than *"a false evil appearing real."* It hindered my ability for years from becoming an effective public speaker and to do the ministry that the Lord has planned for my life.

Besides the fear of public speaking, another reason I could not share my story with an audience was because I would get so full and so emotional when I tried to talk about it. God has been so good to me until I just couldn't tell it all—couldn't talk about all of His goodness, grace and mercy. When I think about the goodness of God and His patience, and all that He has done for my family and me, my soul, my whole being cries out "Hallelujah"! So, when I tried to give my testimony and would cry, my crying was just tears of joy and not tears of pain or sorrow, or fear—as fear was no more an obstacle.

The devil is a liar if he thinks even for a minute that he is going to rob me of this great blessing and opportunity to minister, inspire and encourage others. I know that the Lord has big plans for my life and if Satan can block that blessing he will do everything within his power to do just that. Thanks be to God that no weapon formed against me shall prosper; the weapon will form but, again, it will not prosper. I want others reading this book to overcome their fears by allowing God to be their guide, their walking cane, and refuge—no matter what those fears are. Allow Him to strengthen you and bless you with the power to move onward to greater heights.

I could have given up a long time ago and let fear overtake me and subcome to it; but I decided to take the challenge because I can do all things through Christ Jesus who strengthens me. My confidence in my abilities has grown much stronger over time by just knowing that I have that added power—that added strength to be able to do all the things God has planned for me. The Lord has blessed me to inspire and encourage others, and because I do believe with all the blessings that He has so graciously bestowed upon me, the least I can do in return is to tell others of His goodness, His grace and His mercy. By acknowledging God's Lordship over all of my thoughts, my life, my decisions, and accomplishments, I have learned to be an assertive speaker. I have already overcome the fact that the devil doesn't want me to succeed. This obstacle has been conquered. Victory is mine.

If you wish to overcome the fear of public speaking and if this is one of the areas you feel God is directing you towards to improve your situation, or to share His words and your blessings with others, you too can step out of this fear in order that you may be free to inspire and encourage others to overcome this obstacle also by first confronting the problem head-on. You must first create an impression of authority and strength. Warming up the breath and body by inhaling and exhaling prior to stepping up to the challenge helps you to relax and take in the audience more easier. It also helps to alleviate some of the nervous energy and anxiety that ordinarily comes with speaking in public. Also, your desire and your will to communicate and to inspire others will help you set aside your anxiety and nervousness. Now, don't be confused because I still get butterflies when I first get up to the lectern to speak; however, my fear of speaking in public no longer holds me back and as I get more into my speech and more relaxed, the butterflies flutters in formation and they all fly away perfectly and nicely to an unknown place, high in the sky.

Mental solidity is just as important in public speaking. Knowing the type of audience and why you are giving the speech in the first place, and what your purpose is, gives you a little extra boost and courage to stand tall. Also, to put forth your best efforts to make it the "award winning" speech; or the "testimony" to encourage others and offer hope for them to build upon their own faith makes this obstacle of fear even more worthwhile to overcome. By practicing and persevering, you, too, can learn to speak with confidence, and to speak assertively; whether it be on a particular subject matter, or about christianity. Repetition will enable you to become comfortable doing anything that you weren't comfortable with doing before.

It is knowing that inspiring and encouraging others is the Will of God for our lives that helps us, a lot of the times to learn while doing—and in most cases, this is what it will take to create the rising spiral of self-assuredness and assertiveness that you may desire to conquer when speaking in public.

Finally, it will feel like a breath of hope, and fresh air, after conquering your fears; whether it is public speaking, or any other stumbling blocks that may come into your life. But, through Christ, we can overcome any obstacle that we encounter—with perseverance, practice, and faith in ourselves and in the Almighty.

Remember, now, that God said, *"No weapon formed against us shall prosper."* Only God and we know what our genuine trials and tribulation are. He, too, knows the obstacles we must overcome and He is always available. He's got the whole world in His hands and all we have to do is surrender our burdens upon Him because we, as human beings, are powerless when it comes to overcoming the wickedness of this world solely using our own wisdom and strength. If you are thinking about suicide, abortion, holding a grudge against your parents, your family members, your friends, your co-workers; or whatever the demonic forces may be trying to put into your spirit or your mind to stop you and make your ladder too difficult to climb—just resist such evil intents and lean on the Lord, and Satan won't have a choice but to flee from you; especially when we call upon him to do so in the Name of Jesus. Once he sees that you are not weak enough to play his games and allow him to enter into your spirit, he will go on to the next weakest person and attempt to influence them and draw them into his web—only to destroy their will power, and their opportunity to eternal life, salvation, joy and peace.

We should not let the devil tell us that there is no hope for us, because God has already given us the victory. The generation of curses that the devil has planned for us—well, it stops here and right now with your decision to make a difference in your life and others; because, if we are in the will of God, He will reverse the curse that the devil meant for evil. God tells us in Luke 6:28 that we are to follow His command and that is to, *"Bless them that curse you, and pray for them which despitefully use you."* We are supposed to love our enemies even if they mistreat us. We are supposed to bless them and curse them not; because revenge belongs to God. He also said in Galatians 3:10 that, *"For as many as are of the works of the law are under the curse: for it is written, CURSED IS EVERY ONE THAT CONTINUETH NOT IN ALL THINGS WHICH ARE WRITTEN IN THE BOOK OF THE LAW TO DO THEM."* It is my understanding that if we are believers and obey God's Words and His Laws, we will not be cursed, but protected from all evil for God shall always be with us. "Christ hath redeemed us from the curse of the law, being made a curse for us: for it is written, *"CURSED IS EVERY ONE THAT HANGETH ON A TREE:"* (Gal 3:13). If we are completely obedient to God's word, He will keep us protected and deliver us from evil.

I am overwhelmed with joy in knowing as I do now that what the devil meant for evil in my life, God turned it around for my good. You may be going through something right now that makes it seem like you are cursed and rejected, but hold on because it is really just a process that you must go through that God has planned for your life. God is really blessing you and protecting you from evil. The enemy may mean you some harm; but thank God for Jesus that He will keep you protected. Whatever you are going through, or whatever the situation is, if it's drugs, it it's hate, if it's adultery, it could be a sickness, or you could even be prison bound or have someone you love in prison, it really doesn't matter—God will reverse the curse. God tells us in Deuteronomy 4:30-31 that, *"When thou art in tribulation, and all these things are come upon thee, even in the latter days, if thou turn to the LORD thy God, and shalt be obedient unto his voice; (For the LORD thy God is a merciful God;) he will not forsake thee, neither destroy thee, nor forget the covenant of thy fathers which he sware unto them."* If we continue to stay on the battlefield for the Lord and turn to God for our needs, He will be merciful and restore us with all of the blessings that the devil has taken from us.

Satan thought that he had me bound when things had gotten a little rough on the home front. The curses that the devil thought he had on my family and my relationship with my daughters—God reversed the curse and turned it around for our good. All the peer pressure in the world could not keep us apart because God reversed the curse and gave us the victory over the devil. When I had to declare my seventeen-year old daughter as an adult, I kept the faith and I kept on believing—even when she grew completely out of control to the point where she could no longer live in the family home. When I got divorced, and had to raise three children as a single parent, I kept on believing and trusting in God. When I was so nervous about speaking in public that I could not tell my testimony about the goodness of God and all the things that He had done for me without fear and emotions—I kept on believing and trusting in God.

I thank God everyday because He has placed my feet on solid grounds. He has put a new song in my heart, a new light in my eyes, a new step in my feet and reversed Satan's curse. For my obedience to God, He has turned everything around for my good. God has proven the devil wrong so many times—if you look at my life, and how God has helped me to defeat the devil and his evil ways, you would rejoice with me for every time the devil tried to convince me that I could not do something—God declared victory! God said in Matthew 6:26 that, *"And he saith unto them, why are ye fearful, O ye of little faith? Then he arose, and rebuked the winds and the sea; and there was a great calm."* If you are about God's business, have a little faith in Him, and be obedient to God's Words, He will rebuke the violent storms that come into your life. The results of your persistence to have faith and overcome your trials and tribulations will be a miracle of total calmness, and that little faith will grow from the size of a mustard seed to that which is mature, yet blossoming everyday. Let faith continue to grow in you.

CHAPTER NINE

REAPING THE REWARDS OF FAITH

"Now he that planteth and he that watereth are one: and every man shall receive his own reward according to his own labor." This means that we are God's buildings, God's workers, God's laborers and His servants. We are married to God and we should be in union with Him; therefore, we become laborers together with God, working toward His master plan to build up His Kingdom with those who are faithful to Him. Staying faithful brings Him joy.

I started reaping the rewards of faith as a little girl, I give all the credit to God, my mother and grandmother for the love, support, discipline; and, most importantly, the faith that He, through His holy words and they through their unrelenting courage and wisdom instilled in me and all my sisters and brothers. Now that I am older and wiser—I can reflect back and smile upon some of the memories of growing up, those that were very sweet and those that were bitter, but helped me to develop the wisdom I needed to become who I am today. I can still hear my grandmother singing and praising God throughout the house, late into the midnight hours, and sometimes throughout the day— singing *"The Angels in Heaven Done Signed my Name!"* and *"Amazing Grace, how Sweet the Sound!"* I remember sometimes we would even pretend to be having church in our home. We had a young cousin who would pretend to be preaching the gospel to me, my grandmother, and whoever else was around at the time, and wanted to pretend we were having church. *That same cousin became a minister later in life.* Meanwhile, the rest of us would be having church along with him—just singing and praising God—having a good ole time just glorifying the Lord in the spirit.

In spite of the obstacles in my younger life; my marriage, my family, my professional career; and in sickness, I am still reaping the rewards of faith and leaning on Jesus; because, I have grown so much in the Lord. All of these trials and tribulations were just a test of my faith and has made me stronger in the Lord; and a true believer in miracles. I was being tried in the fire. God has bestowed so much upon me over the years until I just can't even begin to tell you all of it here in these words. But, I thank God for my humble spirit. No matter how high the Lord allows and helps me to go, or how low he takes me, I will always—always be looking up to Him. Proverbs 16:19 says, *"Better it is to be of an humble spirit with the lowly, than to divide the spoil with the proud."* Once I started to follow God's master plan for my life, it did not take me long to catch on and know that God was in charge of my life since I was a young lady, a babe in Christ, and He has completely turned it around for the better over the years. Yes, He turned it around for me and can do the same for you—today. Now that I have come to know; and I have had a taste of God and His goodness, God continues to help me to keep my mind focused on Him, and focused on my purpose in life, my faith and abilities so that the devil can't touch me, nor can he control my life any more. God said, the ones whose mind is stayed on Him, He will keep them in perfect peace. The peace that God is talking about here goes way beyond human comprehension; but, we must lean and depend on God in total confidence, by showing Him that we have faith and trust in Him with our whole heart and being. All of the bad things that happened in my life are what the devil meant for evil, but God turned it around for my good. I belong to God now—He is all around me and He reversed the curse that the devil had "planned" for me and He gave me "victory" over evil with angels to lead and guide me as I walk through life day-by-day. God said He would keep me protected. *"He hath shewed thee, O man, what is good; and what doth the Lord require of thee, but to do justly, and to love mercy, and walk humbly with thy God?"* (Mic 6:7) Yes! He walks with me and He talks to me and will do the same for you when you accept Him into your life as I have done.

Still reaping the rewards of faith, when I was raising my children as a single parent, and like many other working mothers, I struggled and strained to balance my family and my career. I remember when I was trying to obtain my Bachelor's degree; I would take classes at night, take classes during my lunch hour break, and I even took classes on Saturdays so that I could be with my children and support them while bettering my life at the same time. I still found parenting to be a great blessing from God; and at the same time I found it to be a blessing, I also found it to be very challenging. The by-products of all the struggles and strains are my three beautiful mature daughters who are now married and have given me beautiful grandchildren.

In spite of all the trying times and growing pains that we went through, I know that it was the unity, the faith and the prayers sent up to God that moved heaven and kept our family together. I believe that God wants all of us to know that He is in charge of our lives and He is still God, and will always be God no matter what, and that we must remain faithful because without Him we can't make it on our own. We can do nothing without God. It is because of Him that we have use of our physical and mental being. And, for those who are sick or heavy-laden in any manner, God is with them also.

Still reaping the rewards of faith each day, both my husband and I are still trying to get to know each other and balance our careers, which have definitely brought about some challenging times. There were times when I knew we just wanted to throw in the towel, just throw our hands up and say, *"the heck with it all"* walk away from our marriage, and go our separate ways because we couldn't talk and communicate about our issues, nor could we settle our disagreements. Then, one Sunday morning, the Holy Spirit spoke to me and said, "I know your husband is a thorn in your side but until you could show Me that you could live with your thorn, that I had blessed you with, without complaining, I will not pull the thorn out until you could show Me that you have enough faith and trust in Me to work out your problems." Once I could show God that I had enough faith in Him, He would continue to work on my husband's shortcomings so that he would be the husband that He promised me. He has very little patience with people and it seems as though he resents any type of confrontation whether he is right or wrong, he has a very difficult time apologizing when he is wrong. I believe it'll almost kill him to say he's sorry about anything he's done wrong, even when he knows without a doubt that he's wrong or has wronged someone.

However, before God would begin a good work in Lacey's life, I had to first make some changes—I had to humble myself, wait patiently on the Lord and be obedient to His word. The Holy Spirit reminded me that God would pull the thorn out of my side after I proved myself faithful to Him. I had been in an abusive marriage before, and I refused to be involved in another one, be it physically or mentally, because that is not why God put me on this earth. There are times when Lacey would have serious problems in not being able to talk politely to people, he is constantly talking down to them in some of the most rudest tones I had ever seen or heard; sometimes, to the point of total embarrassment. He would often say to me, "God gave me a mouth to talk and I'm gonna yell until He stops me, and I've been yelling all of my life." The only conclusion that I could come up with for the reason he feels that he could talk to people any kind of way is that he has built-up anger over the years that he has to deal with. His anger has nothing to do with me personally, and I don't believe that he does it to try to hurt me. I believe that he is a good-hearted man but he must learn to channel his anger in different directions, or learn new ways of communicating with people without yelling and feeling as though he is justified to do so; because yelling is just not acceptable—we are human beings and must be treated as such—no one wants to be yelled at, nor do they want to be talked down too in a negative way. The Holy Spirit also whispered to me that God said, "He was going to deal with my husband, and that He would fix the problems for us." God wanted me to trust Him with our marriage, and believe that He was going to bring the situations to pass so that we could have the relationship that God had designed it to be. We can't do God's job for Him, all He wants from us is to be patient while He fixes it, and be obedient to His word—have faith in Him and know that He is going to work it out.

God is helping us to work through the growing pains each day. Since we know that our marriage was built on Love and blessed by God, we must wait patiently on the Love Creator to fix the problem.

If God gives you a blessing, He can fix it up and keep it on the right path. If you are experiencing something that you just cannot see your way out, or through it, hold-on until He fixes the problem for you. We know that our marriage takes three—it takes God and the both of us. God said in His words to, "*Cast your burden on the Lord, And He shall sustain you; He shall never permit the righteous to be moved."* When we pour out our grief to God who always remains faithful, we are doing the right thing. God wants us to tell Him all about our troubles. He also wants us to trust Him and He wants us to remain firmly established in life's difficult times. But, we need to put things into the right perspective because we both know that God put us together as one. What we all need to try to do is stop being selfish in all our deeds and put forth the extra effort that is required to work out our differences that causes problems. There must be a lot of giving and a lot of taking in a marriage through communicating, understanding and exercising our faith in God and in each other. The hardest thing about faith is the waiting. We must be patient and wait on the Lord to handle our burdens. I thank God for my faith and being my walking cane to glory. I am also thanking God each day for my husband and allowing us time to know and help each other through life, and all of my other many, many blessings that He has found me worthy of receiving.

Reflecting back on our beautiful wedding day, one of our mementoes to our guests was a bookmark that was titled, "Marriage Takes Three" and it went on to read as follows:

"Marriage Takes Three"
Marriage takes three
To be completed;
It's not enough for
Two to meet.
They must be united
In Love
By Love's Creator,
God above.
A marriage that
Follows God's plan
Takes more than
A woman and a man.
It needs a oneness
That can be
Only from Christ—
Marriage Takes Three.

Through those powerful words, I know, as I always knew by way of God's confirmations that our marriage was built on God's solid ground. Because when Jesus laid down His life and died on the cross, He gave us the perfect example of what true Love is all about. If we only look to God as an example of Love, we can grow into an understanding of what it means to prefer and nurture one another in Love. It is good to have a partner in life and it's even better when a relationship where the both are pulling together, putting the other person first when need be, and going the extra mile to do what it takes to please the other person, but some times when it comes to putting these great intentions into practice, how we find out quickly what a stronghold our own selfish interests have on our hearts and minds. This is when we must remind ourselves of how God intended marriages to be. By God we are brought together with a partner, by faith in God we allow Him to help keep us together. Without God in a marriage—reaping the rewards of faith is surely not to come easy.

We can give God's unconditional and unselfish love to each other as He gives us His empowering strength. Because God is ever-present, we can ask Him for strength and courage as often as we need it throughout each day—no matter where we are—we can always call upon the Lord for help. God is the only way by whom we can have the spots that stain our relationship removed and put back into place to form a wholesome and Holy communion. We know that it is our faith in God that is the foundation of our marriage. Hebrew 3:4 states, "For every house is build by someone, but God is the builder of everything." God also said in Jeremiah that, "For I know the plans I have for you", declares the Lord, "plans to prosper you and not to harm you, plans to give you a hope and a future." He also stated in Lamentation that, "His compassions never fail. They are new every morning; great is your faithfulness."

Love demands that we always say that we are sorry because relationships can't be restored if we can't admit we are wrong or have erred against our love ones. Saying that we are sorry has a lot of power—it has power to keep your relationship and family together. It is extremely hard to admit fallibility, that you are not perfect, or that you have wronged someone but if there is someone out there waiting for an apologize from you, go to them and tell them that you are sorry, and God will help you to express true sorrow for your sins. The first step in recovering from a problem is to acknowledge that you are wrong, accept responsibility—once you acknowledge you're wrong, the healing begins.

Instead of giving up and throwing in the towel as I started to do many, many times—I allowed God to lead and guide me by following His plan. Especially, after I came to know the difference between good and evil; and recognized when the devil was tempting me—so I went all the way and had a lot of talks with God and my guardian angel.

When you are trying to cross your own valleys, swim across your own oceans, cross over your many mountains; or when life takes you to the bottom of the sea, or near to entering a grave and have dirt thrown upon you—snap back, stand back, turn back and go with God all the way, trusting Him to bring you through all of your life's problems—your life's journey. Hallelujah! Lay your head in the bosom of Christ, and pray. Pray every day! Pray every night! Pray all along the way if you must, because prayer fixes things and move mountains out of our way! God states in Thessalonians that, "Pray without ceasing." This scripture means that we should always pray. We are not to lean upon our own understanding but we are to acknowledge God in everything that we think and do, and He will direct our path. There is much joy in faithfulness. The Victory is mine! Saith the Lord! You, too, can experience the joy in serving God and reaping the rewards of faith. The Joy of the Lord is your strength don't let anybody steal it away from you.

It states in the book of Matthews that, *"His Lord said unto him, Well done, thou good and faithful servant: thou hast been faithful over a few things, I will make thee ruler over many things. Enter thou into the joy of thy Lord."*

CHAPTER TEN
SOARING TO NEW HEIGHTS

"But by the grace of God I am what I am: and his grace which was bestowed upon me was not in vain; but I labour more abundantly than they all: yet not I, but the grace of God which was with me." (1 Corinthians 15:10).

When asked, "what is my most significant accomplishment and how has it impacted or affected my life?" I really had to cogitate long and hard about it, because initially I began looking at life itself as a major accomplishment. Being able to survive all the pressures and stresses that come with just living every-day—life was a challenge.

When I became pregnant, I was quickly pegged by some of my family members, and my classmates to be the one less likely to succeed. I am an original. I thank God I'm not like anyone else. I was uniquely made. They had me pegged—they put me in a box—said that I wasn't going to be anything. I wasn't going to mount up to nothing. But, now I'm out of the box they put me in. I'm in the box that my God wants me in. God broke the seal to that box and released His Holy Spirit. I know that I'm out of the box because I have overcome the obstacles that were against me. I knew that I had overcome the obstacles when I could say, "Enough is enough!" to a bad marriage, walked away and never looked back. I have risen above the devil's expectations and soared to new heights. You, too, can get out of the box that you may be in and show the devil that he has no control over your life, your blessings, or your successes. Also, when you do come out of the box, give God some coming out praises. We have to look at everything from God's perspective because if we look at things from our perspective, we are going to mess up big time. God will wreck your plan and over-power it so that you have to be lead by Him. I want to be what God wants me to be. We must always strive to be what God wants us to be. Often we open ourselves up to every imaginable gratification and not allow God to lead or guide us through. We have to change our mind in order to change our spirit to live the life Christ wants us to live. It is not in my spirit that I changed my mind; I changed my life in my mind. It is by the spirit of the Lord processed through faith. Satan feeds our flesh, but God over-powers the devil, and He will feed our mind. The devil will be good to you long enough to get your mind. If he gets your mind, he will keep you down—flesh is too restricted. Once you get to know God, you will get to know yourself because God controls His children and when you come to know the things of God and do His will—God will not limit your potential. You can be broke in your circumstances but rich in your mind. If it is in your mind to overcome what's holding you back in life and in faith, it has to come to pass. Victory is already won! Through all of our trials and tribulations, God teaches us maturity. When we are afflicted—He teaches us to pray!

Another significant accomplishment that helped me to soar to new heights was the fact that I had attained my Bachelor of Science (B.S.) degree in Business Management, but after all the sacrifices and struggles, I was not happy with just a Bachelor degree; because, by the time I had received this degree, it was just like having a high school diploma as everyone had a bachelor's. So I went back to college and attained my Master of Science (M.S.) degree in Human Resource Management. But, when we really think about it, we can have as many degrees as a thermometer and it won't matter or count for helping us get to heaven when we don't have the spirit of God in us. Degrees in education surely won't get you into the Kingdom of God. Because, what is a B.S. degree or M.S. degree without some G.O.D.? Without some G.O.D.—you are lifeless—you are dead in Christ.

I thought about my blessings some more, and the fact that I had raised three beautiful daughters as a single parent, struggled to get my education; I had overcome many obstacles including going in and out of a disturbing marriage; I still kept my faith and spirit up and have lived to tell my story. Surely these events meant that I was soaring to new heights. By the Grace of God, I was able to raise my daughters without them getting on drugs, alcohol or getting pregnant before leaving home and in spite of being tempted by the devil through my family members, we overcame and will continue to soar to new heights. This is truly a blessing and a major accomplishment. It is certainly something that I am extremely proud of.

When I landed my first management job, I thought, *"Hum, I have finally made it to the top."* Wrong! Wrong! Wrong! Don't kid yourself—because management positions are not nearly what they are talked up to be. It is very stressful and it gets extremely lonely up there, and God can see right through you anyway—so if you think being at the top is soaring—think again—unless you are on top for the Lord you have not truly soared.

After thinking back over my life, I know that the management position was not a good analogy or good example to use to show that I had soared to new heights. The Holy Spirit will bring all things back to your remembrance and put it in its right perspective. The Holy Spirit started dealing with me in ways that you cannot even imagine. The Holy Spirit quickened in my spirit, reminding me on a daily basis how the Lord had brought me through all the troubles that had happened in my life—guiding me so that I will not allow them to overtake and consume me. The Holy Spirit reminded me about all of the times that God had healed my body of various illnesses.

I am continuing to soar to new heights because the Holy Spirit gave me the wisdom, knowledge, understanding and inspired me to write these words of inspiration to minister and encourage others through Faith.

Still soaring to new heights, on the other hand, God uses leaders who are faithful. We are most efficient and more effective as a leader when we strive to be faithful rather than trying to be successful by society's standards. God called me to be a leader in my workplace. Some of the ways we can faithfully lead others are being committed to discovering God's will for our life and helping to fulfill it through being a leader. We can also pray for a vision from God and seek His plans for how He would like for us to do and how He would like the people that we lead to be doing. We should articulate clearly, effectively and consistently to others what God's vision and purpose for our life should be. We should commit to building our leadership decisions around God's vision and purpose. Stay focus and continue to communicate with God on a daily basis so that we'll know how He wants us to work toward His vision and lead His people. Also, we should consider what talents God has already given to us to utilize and see how we can best fulfill His purpose in our life. We should seek to set our priorities in alignment to please God rather than trying to please someone else. As the leader God called us to be, we must ensure to set our priorities in such a way that they will enable us to advance the vision God has charged us to do. We should always make time for accomplishing God's vision for us and for the people we lead. We should always without ceasing, motivate, support, inspire and encourage the people we lead and often times, we should challenge them to go beyond their imagination by raising expectations of what we can do together as a team. We should always be willing and ready to listen to the people we lead and try to understand their needs. Stay focus on the vision, keep the faith and don't be sidetracked when crises come into our life. As leaders, we should strive to be the very best mentors we can be by sharing our knowledge, our skills, our values, and our perspectives that will in turn build long-lasting, good relationships. By being the faithful leaders that God has called us to be, we can demonstrate the fruit of the Spirit to the people that we lead which are God's wonderful Love, joy, peace, longsuffering, gentleness, goodness, faithfulness, meekness and temperance. The greatest fruit of all is "Love", and that is something that we can all give.

After becoming employed with the Department of Defense in 1979, I have served in a variety of positions ranging from a GS-2, keypunch operator and film reader, to a GS-13, Chief of the Defense Information Infrastructure (DII) Certification Support Branch. God guided my steps as my bold leadership qualities and intellectual abilities were demonstrated during the development of the DII certification processes and the training awareness tool. Also, the leadership qualities and intellectual abilities were indicative in the implementation of the documented processes that were developed to achieve war fighters' information system requirements. I was picked to lead a team of technical experts to assist and ensure that legacy systems were migrated to the new common operating environment. I took the challenge, with no resources, no policies, no processes, and no procedures in place—just the faith God had put in me. Once we got the resources on board, I lead the team in developing the processes, and provided awareness training to aid customers in their understanding of a new mandated initiative—thereby, enhancing my reputation through the way God made for me, by being able to implement well-documented processes developed under my purview that the war fighters' information systems required.

I have faced a myriad of challenges in my life and in my career with the Government. But, I contributed my success with both of these areas to God and Him blessing me with my leadership skills and abilities to follow through.

I believe because of my faithfulness and leadership qualities, which can only be observed over time—e.g. how I deal with others; how I deal with adversities and complex issues; how I organize my time and efforts; and how I deal with external constituencies is all because God has guided my steps. God said in His words that, "The steps of a good man were ordered by Him." By allowing God's plan to work in my life, He leads and guides me all the way throughout all of my accomplishments. Through Christ Jesus, I believe that I have demonstrated my knowledge, skills and abilities amply over the years. Likewise, I'm not boasting, but I truly believe that I'm more than capable of fulfilling any position or challenge given me because I am blessed with the gifts of faith and God is ordering my steps through life; and I am following His word. I believe through faith that I'm the kind of person such as being that team leader who inspires and encourages others to want to do their very best in whatever they attempt to do.

Everyday, I ask God to give me a balance in my life and strengthen me in my priorities so that I can continue to do the right things and be able to help and inspire others to be motivated enough to move forward on their challenges. Through all the trials and tribulations, it has taken a lot of will power, a lot of praying, a lot of courage, and a lot of faith and trusting God to know that everything was going to be all right. Although, while climbing my mountains hasn't been easy by no means and there have been some very difficult times, my faith in God has been strengthened; and has reassured my trust in Him and caused me to know that God does keep His promises and He is, truly real.

In what I believe have been nothing less than a blessed professional career, I believe that I have remained modest—yet confident, because God made it all possible for me to be where I am in life today. My ability to fit into whatever environment I have been blessed enough to move into has been an essential part of my success and I am glad that I came to recognize when to move on my faith because it's all about faith when soaring to new heights. This is truly my testimony!

How shallow-minded can a person be not knowing when they have "truly" soared to new heights. It is not about all of the material things that we can obtain in life; but it is about our salvation and our relationship with God. Although, I am very proud of all these accomplishments, and they are very beneficial to my family, and me, it was not until I met Jesus, when He saved my soul, and I received the Holy Ghost that I started allowing His words to direct my life. Besides, *I've come to far to turn around,* and if you are waiting on a miracle, perhaps, God has already blessed you with one.

It is great to have those academia degrees from well-known colleges, except I much rather have the degrees that the Lord has conferred on me, which I'm most grateful for. In addition to the academia degrees, I have also graduated with many degrees in the Lord. I graduated from the University of Heaven where I have obtained a **B.A.** degree—I am a **B**orn **A**gain Christian. Thank you lord! I'm a born again Christian who majored in long-suffering and hard knocks. I might not be able to cross all the "T's" and dot all the "I's"; nor speak proper English but, I thank God, He has anointed me. I have obtained a **B.S.** degree also from the University of Heaven—I'm **B**aptized, **S**atisfied and filled with the Holy Ghost! I thank God everyday for my masters' degree in *"Kneeology"*—I have Campbell knees for constantly being on my knees praying, one prayer after another. Finally, I have graduated with the highest degree obtainable in the Lord—I have received my **Ph.D.** degree—God has given me the **P**ower—the **H**oly Ghost power; He has given me **D**eliverance in my soul! You, too, can experience God's abundance of degrees when you start allowing and trusting the Word of God to work directly in your life, your heart, and your spirit—then, that is when you will know, that you know, without a doubt that God is actively involved in your life, directing you, moving you, and guiding you through every step of the way. You will then know that everything is working out according to His purpose and His plan for your life. Everything will be all right. As long as there is breath in your body, it's not too late to live for Jesus.

When the enemy of circumstance seeks to discourage my heart, the Word of God encourages me. When my Faith seems low and weak and my prospects dim, a Word from God renews my Faith and releases a new supply of faith that I need to continue my life's journey. A Word from God ensures success from the moment the Word goes forth. I knew that whatever I wanted, or wanted to do, that I could do it; because, I can do all things through Christ Jesus who strengthens me.

Today, I have Joy, unspeakable Joy! Joy in the morning! Joy in the evening! Joy all night long! I know that the Joy of the Lord is my strength and I refuse to let the enemy, Satan, or anyone else steal my Joy. God gave me this Joy—man surely can't take it away from me! By being a child of God, I can walk upright, with my head up and with confidence because, now, I know who I am in Christ. I don't need man to validate my worth, or try to tell me who I am because I am a new creature in Christ Jesus! I've found what I needed—even though it took a lot of trials and tribulations—I have faith, my family, and I have God on my side.

I believe that I was destined to soar through my many adversities of life and reach new heights in God, so that when God brought me through my troubles, I could share my triumphs with the world by being that teacher of faith through these messages and lessons in life as directed, implemented and inspired of God for the purpose of bringing others up His throne with me. I also believe that you, too, are destined to soar to new heights, and any other person that allows God's plan to work in their lives. God gives my body the release it needs. He gives my mind and soul a beautiful melody and my spirit a wonderful gust of wind that makes me bold, beautiful and able to soar to new heights. God said, *"they that wait upon the Lord shall renew their strength; they shall mount up with wings as eagles; they shall run, and not be weary; and they shall walk and not faint."*

When you feel all of life crushing down on you and you cannot go another step, just remember that you can call upon the Lord to renew your strength.

When we wait upon the Lord, we are expecting God's promised strength to help us rise above our life's distractions, trials, tribulations and difficulties. We must wait on the Lord, and be patient when He asks us to wait, and expect Him to fulfill the promises that we read about in His Words—the B.I.B.L.E.

I soared from an uneducated single parent to an educated child of God! I struggled and strained for many years trying to find peace and harmony within me that only God could give. He said in His word that the ones whose mind stays on Him, He would keep them in perfect peace. I was looking for peace in all of the wrong places. I was thirsty for righteousness and was truly in need of Gods word. I had begun to experience a deep desire for personal righteousness, which was proof of my spiritual rebirth and growth in the Lord. It tells us in Matthew 5 that, "Blessed are they which do hunger and thirst after righteous: for they shall be filled."

The highest height in my life was when God saved me and changed my life. It is that wonderful relationship that I have with my Heavenly Father and my journey with Him that allows me to continue to spiritually soar. Now, that I am a changed person—a new creature in Christ, I think differently, I'm more caring, loving, more meek, patient, and supportive of others. It brings me great joy and rewards when I'm focused and doing what I know that I'm called and drawn to do, which is the Will of God and a messenger of testimonies over faith through which all thing are possible. It was quite evident to me when I noticed how much I had soared in my walk with God, how strong my belief in God had gotten and my relationship with Him. Because, I know how to walk with Him better than I did when I was *"just going to church."* I have a personal relationship with God and that is why I feel that I am truly soaring to new heights—something that I did not have before; and that is how I also knew that I had a friend in Jesus. Let us not make any mistakes, this road has not been easy, nor has it been perfect, nor will yours be; but keep holding on. I have encountered many bumps along the way; however, I fought like a champion and stayed on the battlefield for the Lord because I knew He was my rock, my shield, and my shelter in that mighty storm of life, and He is my walking cane to glory. I know that He is not asking me to do anything—God is commanding me to continue to do His Will; therefore, I expect many, many more bumps on this journey for the Lord as I've only just begun the rest of my journey. God has opened doors for me that had previously been closed in my face. Thank you Jesus! He has offered me opportunities of a lifetime, and they are mines just for the taking. He said that, *"we have not, because we ask not."* God gave me that balance in my life that I needed to stay on track with Him. He keeps me focused on Him and He reminds me constantly of the things that He has done for me during the course of my life, and my soul rejoices just knowing all of His goodness, grace and mercy that He has so graciously bestowed upon me. Although, I worked extremely hard, it was the grace of God that enabled me to accomplish all that I did. Thank you Lord for allowing me to be able to soar to new heights of this magnitude and to help others to come into recognition of their own potential, courage, and faith even if it may be as small as a grain of mustard seed.

Today, I look forward to entering into the Kingdom of God when I am called up to meet Him. I look forward to wearing my golden crown because I will have earned it, fair and square. Riding high! At times I feel as though I'm on top of the world, high above all the crowds, this proud Child of God enjoys the closeness and warmth of her relationship with her Heavenly Father at its best.

"And suddenly a voice came from heaven, saying, 'This is my beloved Son, in whom I am well pleased'". (Matthew 3:17)

Thank God that I am a Christian. I like to share the following poem with you. I don't believe I could have put it any better or could make it any clearer. Enjoy!

When I Say "I Am A Christian"
When I say..."I am a Christian"
I'm not shouting "I am saved"
I'm whispering "I get lost!"
"That is why I chose this way."

When I say..."I am a Christian"
I don't speak of this with pride.
I'm confessing that I stumble
and need someone to be my guide.

When I say..."I am a Christian"
I'm not trying to be strong.
I'm professing that I'm weak
and pray for strength to carry on.

When I say..."I am a Christian"
I'm not bragging of success.
I'm admitting I have failed
and cannot ever pay the debt.

When I say..."I am a Christian"
I'm not claiming to be perfect,
my flaws are too visible
but God believes I'm worth it.

When I say..."I am a Christian"
I still feel the sting of pain
I have my share of heartaches
which is why I seek His name.

When I say..."I am a Christian"
I do not wish to judge.
I have no authority.

Carol Wimmer

CHAPTER ELEVEN

DISCOVERING YOUR TRUE DESTINY

Now that you are aware of how to soar to new heights, have you discovered your true destiny as I have mine? Do you know where you are headed; or are you just standing in limbo waiting for someone to coach you through life? Often people have to be coached, to be encouraged to keep going, or to persevere. Do you know what kingdom you belong to? Earthly or eternally? Perhaps, you probably have heard that your destiny was predetermined before you were born, and if that is true—and I believe that it is—why fight God's master plan for your life—just allow Him to show you the way to discovering your true destiny. God said, "For whom he did foreknow, he also did predestinate to be conformed to the image of his son, that he might be the first-born among many brethren." When trying to acquire the right vision, seek God's plan, because He has already given you a vision.

Since nothing can be hidden from God, He has complete knowledge of all things—all you do, say and think. He had determined from eternity, before we were born, to bring His chosen few into a special relationship with Himself. We were foreordained and conformed to the image of God.

To help you discover your vision in order to realize your true destiny, I would like to recommend that you began immediately to follow God's plan for your life. To discover your true destiny, God said, *"Seek ye first the kingdom of God and His righteousness, and all these other things shall be added unto you."*

Seek God's rulership over your life. God has rules that must be followed in order for us to enter into His kingdom. First, we must be obedient to His word and allow the Holy Spirit to lead and guide us through this earthly journey until God calls us to our heavenly home. Next, we need to understand that there are two groups of people—*Kingdom people* and *worldly people*; but there is a big difference in these two groups of people. Both have kingdoms; however, we must ensure that we are destined for the right kingdom, which is God's Kingdom, and God will give you the values that you are seeking and the blessings that you are in need of. He will help you find your treasures in life when you become a seeker of His Kingdom and make it your goal to focus on. There is no guarantee that everyone will be blessed as there is no guarantee that everyone's faith will be strong enough to follow through; but if you believe strong enough and truly turn it all over to God, you will know for yourself, in your heart, in your own mind when you are being blessed and working towards God's Kingdom.

The worldly people, on the other hand, will have you believing that your kingdom is in the "stuff" that you are accumulating on earth. They will also have you idolizing the car that you are driving. They will have you idolizing the house that you are living in, the money that you are spending and the job that you get up everyday to go to without giving God His thanks and His glory for blessing you with the "stuff" that you are enjoying everyday. We are "stuff" motivated, and we don't give God the glory and the praises that He deserves for blessing us to be able to get the "stuff", and enjoy it and often we think we did it all by ourselves.

Further, the worldly people, or society in general, especially those who seek wealth as their salvation will have you disliking yourself. They will have you comparing yourself to other worldly wealthy people, and if you are not doing as well as they are, and not living in a luxury home, and driving an expensive car, then you are labeled in a category with what they call "low class citizens" and "unsuccessful." Some of the elites will even go as far as to say that you are "poverty stricken." Thereby, not fitting in with the higher echelons of your own community—the elites, or esteemed groups, if you will.

Even if you choose God and the eternal treasures as your wealth, life will still seem so unfair by the standards of humankind. God will sometimes put you in some very uncomfortable positions, places and situations to help you become more obedient to Him before He starts blessing you. You may think that you don't have very much right now by society standards. Perhaps, you may even think that you are truly living in poverty, when God is, on the other hand, through the storms and rain, only trying to show you how to trust in Him in all of your ways and lean not unto your own understanding. This is all part of the process, the training and discipline that you must go through in order to reign with God later. God said, *"commit our ways unto Him, trust in him and He shall bring it to past."* God may sometimes have your car taken away from you, so that you have to walk places where you would not normally walk only to cross someone's path to minister to them, because you probably wouldn't go otherwise. He may even fix it so that you can't pay your bills just so that you can share that testimony and encourage someone else to hold-on and not to give up. God may also fix it from time to time where you cannot even buy food to eat just so that you can go out to look for food just to end up ministering to a child in need, or seeing how people are without and hungry. God sometimes even makes us homeless just to minister to the homeless because all of that is Kingdom's business—it is the Will of God—it is Kingdom's ministry.

There will be times and things that God will tell us to do that seems totally out in left field, and off the wall. We won't even understand why we have to do certain things, and probably don't even want to—but we are led to do it anyway; and we need to do it because, we need to be obedient to the Word of God.

Poverty is not just being without money, shelter or food, but it is also being of a poor mind and lack of joy and contentment in our spirit. We can have other forms of poverty by allowing the worldly people to rob us of many riches in our life that are far more important and more valuable than material things, riches like the Holy Spirit and confidence in seeking the Kingdom of God. We should not let Satan push or introduce us into that type of poverty. If we allow Satan to rob us of our minds where we can't think, then we have 'poverty of the mind.' The goals and dreams that we have set for ourselves will never be attained if we allow poverty of the mind to set in. The joy of the Lord is our strength and our answer to all heavenly blessings. Therefore, we can't have strength without joy, so, if we allow Satan to take away our joy, we become very weak in the mind to the point that we can't even fight off the devil—consequently, we have created 'poverty of joy'. If our Joy has been weakened, then we need to ask God to come in and renew it—to give us a fresh supply of his great Joy! We need this renewed and fresh supply of joy because, we have allowed Satan to take control over our lives and steal our joy, as he is not just a motivator of sin, but a thief as well. When our goals and dreams have fallen through the cracks, we walk around depressed, alone, no happiness in our lives, and no hope; and, the only person that is happy is the devil. If we become low in our spirit, where we don't allow the holy spirit to lead and guide our directions in life anymore, then our spirit becomes poverty stricken because now we are letting Satan rule our lives. We are no longer seeking God's kingdom first and we have taken our eyes off of God's plan for our lives. But, this is exactly what Satan wants us to do. As long as he thinks that he is in control and has defeated us, he is happy and we are sad, and he starts seeking, to and fro, for his next weakest victim to devour.

The devil's job and goals are to steal, kill and destroy. If we allow the devil to rob us of our minds, joy, spirit, power, and strength, we become very vulnerable and susceptible to him. Also, we become poverty stricken in all of those areas with no power to fight him back—giving him the power over our lives to totally rule and do whatever he wants to do to us. We often pass this down through our families even for generations, by not recognizing when he has us where he wants us—he has us under his control. Our children will sometimes take on the same spirit, inheriting the curse-poverty in the spirit and, thus, weakened in their faith.

On the other hand, by choosing God's plan for our lives to discover our true destiny, He will break the spirit of poverty off our lives. Whatever that power is over us that is causing us not to be able to get closer to God—it can be broken—we just need to let go and let God lead and guide us through our journey to discover our true destiny by trusting and becoming more knowledgeable of His words.

If God is for us, it is worth more than the whole world against us. Amen! The Victory is ours—Thank God for the victory! Amen! He said in His words that He will rebuke the devour for our sake. No weapon formed against us shall prosper if we are in His will. Again, the weapons will form however; but God won't allow them to prosper. Your enemies will become your footstool, and life just keeps getting better, and we just sit back, relax, and enjoy our blessings and the joy, which the world, nor Satan will ever be able to take away.

When we look at how society views us in terms of how we should fit in it, and not look at how God views us, in turns of what we must do, then we truly need to ask ourselves, *"Where is my heart"?* Because the Word of God says, *"For where your treasure is, there your heart will be also."* That is why it is so very important to know what Kingdom you belong to. The choice to choose between earthly and eternal treasures is totally up to us as God puts wisdom in each of us to know the difference. However, we cannot have two masters—We cannot serve God and riches—God is a jealous God—you must choose one or the other. You must be either cold or hot with God because He said in His Word that if we're lukewarm He will spew us out of His mouth; because of the lack of genuine faith we show in Him. God views us as worthless when we are lukewarm and are not sure of which side of the fence we should be on. God is real, and He can tell when we are not genuine. We must repent of our lack of genuine faith and spiritual understanding to receive the blessings that God has for us. If we choose the earthly treasures, when we die, we can't take the "stuff" with us. The worldly people that we leave behind will argue and fight over our "stuff", that we have worked so hard to get all of our life. I once read a quote that said, "What I hoard, I lose: but what I give, I keep." There is a lot of truth to that statement, we don't want to be greedy and not share with others what God has blessed us with—we are blessed so that we can bless others. We can't take our earthly treasures with us when we die, but we can send them on ahead by sharing with others some of the blessings that God has bestowed upon us; and continue supporting Kingdom's work. If your riches are here on earth, your heart will be bound to this world's system, but only for a short while. If your riches are in heaven, you will seek those things that are above and use the things of this world to glorify God because it is in your heart and in your spirit to do so. You don't want to lay up treasures here on earth where the moth and rust destroys them; nor where thieves break in your house and steal all of your treasures while your soul is lost. You want to lay all of your treasures up in heaven where the moth; nor rust destroys, and the thieves don't break in to steal your treasures; we should use worldly treasures only to get us by and supply only our earthly needs while helping others—keeping in mind that God knows and sees our future and wants us to expand beyond our imagination. However, other people and our friends can only see us right here and now—our present; and they are quite happy with us just the way we are and where we are in life.

Only the visionaries grow in the Kingdom. The light will also shine more in your life if you are in the Will of God. Also, I am very glad for what He has blessed me with, whether it will be supplying all my earthly needs or heavenly needs and I shall press on like a Christian soldier should and not depend upon society to guide or direct me. What may appear to be poverty in society eyes; however, may truly be a blessing to someone else; because, it is all part of God's plan for us to be just where we are today in life. God will supply all of our needs while we are on our journey to discover our true destiny. God said in His word that, "He wouldn't leave us; nor would He forsake us." God also tells us in His words, "To be not wise in thine own eyes, and for us to fear the Lord, and to depart from evil."

If you are going to fulfill your true destiny, you got to make some changes. There must be some type of change in your life. You can't go into your future until you stop looking back into your past. No more looking back. It's time to start a new beginning. If the worldly people are hindering you from getting closer to God, you need to flee from them so that you can receive your blessings. God went on to say that, *"But the eyes of the wicked shall fail, and they shall not escape, and their hope shall be as the giving up of the ghost."* We must be careful not to think to highly of our earthly possessions because God also told us that, *"It is easier for a camel to go through the eye of a needle, than for a rich man to enter into the Kingdom of God."*

CHAPTER TWELVE

TESTIMONIES OF MY FAITH

Webster states that, "a testimony is bearing witness to the truth, evidence, proof, or first hand authentication of a fact." I have often heard that you can't have a testimony without being tested because you have to go through some pains, sorrows, trials and tribulations before you can tell someone else what you've gone through and how God brought you out. It is through your personal experiences with God, you share the truth that has come to you first-hand.

Often as we walk through life, going from one event to another, one trial and tribulation to another, we never look back, or stand up and testify about what the Lord has done for us. Sometimes we just take life for granted until some distressing events happens, such as a death of a family member, a terminal illness, or lost of a job; but, we must be ready to do the right thing at all times and tell somebody else about God's goodness—all the things that He has brought us through.

The sharing of your personal testimony is more effective in drawing others closer to Christ. It catches the attention of the unbelievers and could sometimes hold their interest. A personal testimony is unique because it describes your personal life, your personal experience and your personal relationship with God before and after you received Christ and how He dealt with you personally in drawing you closer to Him.

My grandmother always wanted me to be a teacher; but I believe she would have settled for any of her children or grandchildren to become a teacher. However, since I did not step up to the challenge, I feel that since there is a lesson to be learned in these messages I'm sending through these pages, just maybe, my grandmother got her teacher after all—just not in the classroom environment. I pray everyday that my grandmother is looking down upon us, upon me, with a great big smile as she did so beautifully to brighten our day. Also, I hope that she is rejoicing in the Lord knowing that she not only has one teacher, but she has many teachers spreading the "good news", because God's way is a way that we can't go around. Furthermore, this lesson is for all the ones who would like to experience God's love and His goodness in their lives.

I went through life for many, many years swearing that I would never step foot in another school or college again. Never say never! In December of 1986, I graduated from college swearing that I would never, ever, step foot inside of another college as long as I lived; because, it took me nearly nine years to finish my undergraduate studies. It was very difficult working a full-time job everyday, raising three children as a single parent, trying to maintain a household and going to college at night and on Saturdays for a very long time. However, being a child of God, with a renewed spirit, in 1993, with much prayer and the desire to want to further develop my life, my education and my career, I decided that I wanted to go back to college. In the spring of 1993, I enrolled with Troy State University. I wanted to start early in 1993; however, I discovered that I had inadvertently made a $300.00 mistake in my checkbook, so I knew that I personally couldn't afford to go that quarter. Thus, I prayed to God, and I told Him that I believed that it was He who had opened the door of opportunities for me to go back to college. I didn't believe that God had brought me that far to leave me there, or that He would allow the doors to close at that point. Within a couple of weeks, I received a monetary performance award for approximately $300.00. God is good, because that mistake I made in my checkbook was quickly recovered. Thank You God!

The blessings just kept on coming. A couple of weeks after the performance award, I received another check in the mail in the amount of $1,144.00, which I truly did not expect to receive because the time allotted for me to receive that check had expired. This was just another sign to show the world, and me that God's time is totally different from man's time. Shortly after that, I received a letter from the career's program office congratulating me on being approved for tuition assistance and stating that money had been budgeted and set aside for me to attend college. However, the only stipulation with receiving the tuition assistance was that I had to maintain a 'B' average, which I did. Today, I hold a Master's Degree, in Human Resource Management.

It is my job to tell you that if God has a blessing for you, no one can take it away from you, no one can stop it, and you will receive it. It may not come when you want it to come but it's always on time, but once it happens, you should tell somebody—share it as appropriately as possible; because, it is your testimony, and it could be just what the unbeliever needs to hear to strengthen their faith in God to make that change in their life.

In spite of all the stumbling blocks, I knew if it was God's Will for me to go back to college that He would supply my needs and give me the desires of my heart. I will bless the Lord at all times; Praises to Him shall continually be in my mouth.

Still praising God for His goodness, His grace and His mercy. He has healed my body of illnesses. I was born an asthmatic. For ten long years I suffered with chronic asthma with no real cure. I remember my older sisters and brothers telling me how sick I use to be as a child growing up with asthma—walking around the house very chubby and could hardly breathe. I use to wheeze so badly; grasping for air, often having asthma attacks such that I had to be hospitalized—and not knowing if I would make it back home alive. Thanks and praises be to God as He healed my body from asthma, and there are no signs of asthma recurring.

In September 1991, I was hospitalized for the doctor to determine why I was experiencing excruciating pain in my neck, in my back and what was causing my right side to go numb. At times it would go paralyze on me. They performed a myelogram to diagnose the problem. A myelogram is a procedure that is performed with a needle and iodine, where the doctor drew spinal fluid from my back to make room to inject the iodine to assist him in accurately diagnosing the problem. The doctor informed me after analyzing my diagnosis that he had found the problem—three herniated disks located in my cervical spine area. He also told me how he planned to correct the problem with surgery. As the doctor began telling me all the things he was going to do to correct the herniated disks, he was also preparing me for surgery as he stated that, "it was normal procedures and/or normal practice, once he received the results of the myelogram, to perform the surgery while the patient was still in the hospital." However, after lying there flat on my back, and with much prayer, I told the doctor that it was not yet time for me to undergo surgery; because, I didn't believe that the Lord was ready for me to have the surgery. So, the doctor released me from the hospital the very next day, and told me that he was going to write me a prescription for painkillers. He also said that he would continue to write prescriptions until I decided to have the surgery because where the herniated disks were located, I would not be able to function normally, nor would I be able to bear the pain without medication. Once I was out of the hospital and kept praying, God basically took away the pain and I barely experienced any discomfort from my herniated disks. Today, many years later, Glory be God, there has been no surgery and no more painkillers. Thank you Jesus! God tells us in Isaiah that, _"He was wounded for our transgressions, he was bruised for our iniquities: the chastisement of our peace was upon him; and with his stripes we are healed."_ He has also borne our grief. He personally suffered severe pain from the torture of the crucifixion upon the cross so that we who are servants of His don't have to suffer. He suffered so I wouldn't have too.

On the morning of 11 September 1998, I was on my way to State Farm Insurance Company, in Fairborn, Ohio, to buy homeowners insurance for a new home that the Lord had blessed us to have built from the ground up. I prayed on the way to State Farm, asking the Lord to let LOGTEC Incorporated call my husband that day for a job so that he could assist in providing financial support to the family household. Approximately 4:20 P.M., that very same day, an employee of the company called. I answered the phone and he asked for Lacey. I told him that Lacey was not home at the moment; but I would take a message, and have him call once he returned home. I also asked the employee if they were going to hire Lacey in their company. The employee told me, "yes"—that they had six vacancies and that they wanted to give him one of them. However, when Lacey returned the call, it was to no avail, as he did not get either one of those jobs. I guess I just asked God to let the company call him and they did call him that day. What I should have asked God for was to have the company call and offer him a job. So you really need to be careful in the "way" that you ask God for things, because most of the time you will get just what you ask Him for. God has an awesome sense of humor. If you want to see God laugh just try making plans without Him, and watch how quickly He changes it. The company did call just as I 'd prayed for them too and that was it—no job, just the call. Then, I had to go back in prayer and ask God to have the company to call him again and offer him the job, which was also the desire of Lacey's heart.

God is so good and so true to His word. You just have to believe and have faith in God to bring that blessing to pass, be patient, wait and He will do the rest. When it looks impossible for man that's when it is just right for God. He said to commit our ways unto Him, trust in Him and He will bring it to pass. Whatever the situation is, God can and will fix it for us in His own time—not our time but His time; furthermore, His ways are neither like our ways nor His thoughts like our thoughts. I had no doubt that Lacey would get hired with the company. However, a couple of days later they called back and said that the jobs were there but the customer didn't have the money allocated to pay for the work; and that they were in a wait mode until they could work out the financial issues. In the meantime, while Lacey was waiting to be called, he patiently worked several odd jobs for various department stores in the local area.

In November 1998, Lacey finally interviewed for a job with the company, we thought that this was it. This was finally going to be the breakthrough that we had been waiting for—the job that we had been waiting so long for; but again he didn't get the job. Another person was selected for the position; after I had prayed so hard for Lacey to be blessed with the job, an overwhelming feeling came over me. It was as though God Himself had said, "it's his job," and I felt a peace about the job being his—a calming peace of assurance. Although he did not get the job, I still thanked God everyday for blessing Lacey as though he had already gotten the job; and whenever someone would ask if he had gotten the job, I would always, always respond—"not yet, but it's coming." I believed with all my heart that God was truly going to come through for Lacey, for us.

Approximately five months later, on 13 April 1999, he finally got the long awaited phone call from the company, and on 14 April 1999, he started working for them. This is the same position that he had interviewed for in November 1998; and he was not selected at the time. The guy they had selected worked only a short while and later left the position for another job within the company, leaving the position vacant once again. You see, we did get the blessing for my family's financial support. In spite of how difficult the situation seemed from the human eye, receiving this blessing just goes to show you that you can't beat God's givings, no matter how hard you try. If you've got something you need God to take care of for you, you have only to ask. God said, "You have not, because you asked not." He went on to say, "And whatsoever ye shall ask in my name, that will I do, that the Father may be glorified in the Son. If ye shall ask any thing in my name, I will do it." I strongly believe that when God has your name on a blessing, no one can take it from you. They can have it delayed; but they can't take your blessings away from you. Praise the Lord!

Just when I thought I had finished writing my book, this old wicked world threw me another crooked curve ball. My life has taken a roller coaster ride for months in and months out. Early July 2000, my mother was stricken with pneumonia. If you know anything about the love for your mother, I know that you know at that moment we all panicked when we heard the news because our mother had never been sick enough for us to be concerned. Then, just before my mother could completely recover from her illness, a couple of weeks after that, a mysterious incident happened, some cold hearted, evil spirited person killed my sister in cold blood, and left the scene to never show their face again. Why would someone want to kill somebody who wouldn't even think about killing a flea—I would never know? Why would someone want to take my mother's child's life? My sister's life! To take someone else's life, or someone else child's life is an evil deed. We probably will never know or ever understand what happened. My mother would help anybody in the world but I don't think her payback should have been for somebody to rob her of her precious child—the child God blessed her with—leaving my mother to grieve herself to death because of the loss of her child. Yet again, approximately three weeks after the mysterious death of my sister, my mother falls into more tragedy, she had now fallen, broken her hip and had to have hip surgery, which took several months to recover, which she never did fully recover.

Again, I was thrown another curve, exactly two months later, my mother's brother, and my favorite uncle died and now, again, we have another set back that we must overcome. For a while, it appeared that every month for one reason or another we were experiencing some type of tragedy in our family—one stumbling block after another, one trial and tribulation after another. I believed that God was truly testing my faith.

Here again, in Dec 2000, my mother's kidneys failed her and had to be put on permanent dialysis. A couple of weeks later, she had congestive heart failure, then her lungs collapsed. Through all of the tragedies and losses, I continued to pray and trust God to bring my mother through her illness, to heal and restore her body; all the while I remained faithful, hoping that He would strengthened her body. Now, God is really putting my faith through a serious test. I know God is still on the throne and working on me. He is still testing my faith to see if I truly have the relationship with Him that I confess to have. He is trying to see if I still trusted Him in spite of my losses, in spite of all my trials and tribulations.

The biggest test of all, for me, came in mid-February 2001, during the President's Day weekend, we started our journey south to Florida to see my mother because she had been ill. At this point, we knew she had been ill for quite some time, approximately two months, so we decided to go see her, so, the first opportunity we got, we headed south. We wanted to get there sooner; however, we had custody of our grand baby who was living with us at the time and we didn't want her to miss too much school. Furthermore, things seemed to have been improving with my mother's health and things appeared to be looking brighter. We believed that because we had recently received a phone call the day before telling us they had moved her from the Intensive Care Unit (ICU) into a regular room.

Just days before we journeyed south, I had spoken on her behalf, at church, during Altar Prayer. I mentioned that we had received a phone call stating she had slipped away. She had died! The Doctors had brought her back a couple of times before and they were afraid if it happened again they would break her ribs because at that point, she had lost a lot of weight and was very fragile. The hospital staff wanted the family to make a decision on whether or not the staff should attempt to save her and try to bring her back if she flat-lined again. I told my sister that my mother was in her right mind and could make her own decisions whether or not she wanted the hospital staff to continue to try to save her life. I felt that it was the Lord who revived her before and it was His decision to take her, and not the great work of the Doctors. I, then, asked for prayer from our Church family and friends.

We started our trip early around 4 A.M. While we lived in Ohio, we had made this journey several times, usually we would stop in Montgomery, AL., visit either my sister or my husband's family and then continue on to Florida which was approximately another three-hour drive. However, this particular trip, I didn't have a good feeling when I left home that morning, so this time we didn't stop in Montgomery, we decided to go straight to the hospital, which is located in Pensacola, Florida.

We arrived in Pensacola around 5:45 P.M. We were extremely tired; we parked the van and went straight up to her room. As we approached her room, my nephew, Larry, was running hastily through the doors, from my mother's room as though she had already died, almost knocking me over, saying, "It's killing me to see my grandmother this way, in that condition." As we entered the room, we noticed she had visitors, my sister-in-law, two nephews and a niece, while they were trying to settle her down, she was fiercely fighting to take the oxygen mask out of her nose, and unplugging her self from the various tubes and/or machines she was hooked up to. She finally recognized Lacey, Jamesia, and me were in the room. She immediately wanted a hug from everyone in the room. We all hugged her and gave her a kiss. She had one of my nephews fanning her while she repeatedly said she was burning up and wanted us to keep fanning her. She finally calmed down, we had a visit from her nurse, and I had several questions for the nurse about all the dried blood on my mother's clothing along with other concerns. They got her all cleaned up and she seemed too be resting find at this point. However her body was cold as ice, which was normal after she would finish her Dialysis treatment. She had a heating machine over her body in an effort to bring her body temperature back up to normal body temperature. I attempted in assisting my nephew to cooling her off also by fanning her body because she said that she was burning up, the more we fanned her, the hotter she got. A male nurse entered the room and posed a question to her, he asked, "Mrs. Jackson, do you know where you are?"

She replied, "Yeah, um in heaven! Ya'll gonna join me ain't cha?"

We responded saying, "Yes, Ma'am."

He, the nurse, walked out of her room, and moments later, I noticed the gauges on the machine showing some very strange numbers, extremely low numbers—the machine wasn't responding at all. I took my hand and moved it across her face, back and forth, calling her name, there was no movement, no response, or activity from her. Her eyes were cocked wide-opened, looking upward toward the ceiling. I left the room to get a nurse who was supposed to have been monitoring my mother's condition from the nurse's station. She rushed in the room, checked her condition—all of her vital signs, and then, asked the family to leave the room. Moments later I walked back into the room to check on her status, and heard the one nurse call for a, "code blue." At that time, I slowly turned around, walked out of the room, softly telling the family members I just over heard the nurse call a code blue on my mother, and I responded to my family by saying, "they better hurry up and get some help in there to save my mother."

A few moments later, the hospital Chaplain came in, and introduced herself to our family. Then, you can see and hear about fifteen to twenty hospital staff personnel running and rushing into her room. The door to her room is now wide open and I entered the room again. At this point I was getting a little upset because the door was opened wide and they had my mother lying in bed, with only her hospital gown on, her gown pulled up and opened to the side, exposing all of her flesh for the world to pass by to see. I asked them to close the door. If they had planned to keep the door opened, at least cover her up until they were ready to check her status because she deserved far more respect than they were giving her. My mother was a lady of grace and with much dignity. They covered her body and again asked me to leave the room because they didn't think I would be strong enough to take seeing the procedures they were about to perform. The hospital staff stated it wouldn't be a pretty sight, and they would rather I go to the waiting room next door, and wait until they could inform us of her progress. So we went to the room next door in an attempt to wait, after about eight to ten minutes, I decided to leave the room for a private prayer. My husband suggested to the Chaplain that it would be a good idea if we could all pray together.

We took a trip downstairs, out the door, in front of the hospital, where there were five of us in a circle, the Chaplain opened with a prayer, as she finished I continued the prayer, followed by one of my nephews, Dino, and my husband ended the prayer circle. There were some powerful praying going on in front of the hospital, people were passing by wondering what was going on. As we were all walking back to my mother's room you could feel the holy spirit as we all knew everything was going to be all right; because right after we prayed, it was an overwhelming spirit that came over me, telling me not yet my child. It was not yet time for my mother to go. As we quietly returned back upstairs, next door to my mother's room where the staff continued to work on her, we sat there talking with the other family members, still praising God for the blessings of keeping my mother alive.

You know the devil was still at work, again, you must remember his job is to steal, kill and destroy, and boy was he ever on his job that evening. As we all sat patiently and calmly in the room next door, about ten minutes later you could see some of the medical staff personnel slowly leaving the room, their heads hung down, not looking very happy, removing their gloves and shaking their heads from side to side as to indicated that my mother was gone—she was dead. Once my nephew, Larry, looked at one of the nurses, as she exited my mother's room, she looked back at him and moved her head from side to side, you could tell that he did not want to hear what the hospital staff had to say, so he took off running, and in a loud voice he said, "How am I gonna tell my mother that her mother is dead." My other nephew, Dino immediately followed him. My husband went to find them to ensure they were okay—he found them holding up each other in a hugging like manner. When he returned to the room the Chaplain was there again telling me that the Doctor would be out soon with some news and to be prepared for the worse. She had just left out of the room where my mother was and knew exactly what the doctor was about to tell us. She quickly reminded me of the prayers we had prayed earlier. Shortly, the doctor arrived in the room where we were waiting, next door, told us that, "she's gone—she's dead!" He stated that she was too weak for them to bring her back, and they were afraid to put any more pressure on her little fragile body. Three times, I asked the doctor who was in charge, if he had truly done everything he could do for my mother?

He replied, "yes."

I then turned to his nurse, asked her the same question. Her reply was the same, "yes, she replied."

At that moment, I stood outside of my mother's room, and started screaming. I cried out Lord, "You said not yet my child." I began screaming, "No Jesus! No Jesus! No! No Jesus! No Jesus! No"! The chaplain tried to intervene again by reminding me of the prayers we had prayed earlier.

She told me that, "My prayers almost reached heaven." When she told me that my prayers almost reached heaven, at that point, I felt that she needed prayer because it appeared that she didn't have enough faith in God to bring my mother through. I really didn't want her around me anymore trying to shake my faith or put doubt in my mind because she believed that my prayers didn't reach heaven, nor did she believe me when I told her that God had spoken to me and said not yet my child.

I told her that, "My prayer did reach heaven because God had told me not yet my child."

The chaplain told me that, "I might as well accept the fact that she is gone, she is dead."

I told the Chaplain, "It was not God's Will for my mother to die—it wasn't her time to go, at least not right now."

The Chaplain again said, "You said, you were going to accept God's Will, you heard the doctor, he said that your mother is dead, accept it."

I continued to scream and cry out to the Lord for my mother. I was challenging God, going back and forth, telling Him that He had just spoken to me earlier and said not yet my child; I collapsed in the hallway from the exhaustion of screaming and crying out to the Lord. When I had come to, I found myself in a wheelchair. At this point, I got up out the wheelchair, my husband saw that I was okay, and he went to find my two nephews to tell them about the sad news that we had just received from the doctor and his staff. He found them in a waiting room down the hall, and around the corner. My husband told my nephews what the doctor had just told us, they hugged each other and begin to cry. As he was headed back to the room where I was, he informed some of the nurses that my nephews were in the waiting room around the corner and appeared to be in need of some consoling because of the devastating news they had just received. When my husband arrived back into the room where I await-ed him, I was talking with one of the doctors who was informing me that they were going to clean my mother up, and let us see her just before they prepare to take her to the morgue. Still, not believing that she was dead.

While waiting for the doctor to return to the waiting room to let us know that it was now okay to go back in her room before taking her to the morgue, my husband leaves the room to go back down the hall, and around the corner to check on my Nephews to inform them if they would like they could see her before they took her to the morgue. At this point, two nurses are consoling my nephews as they walked back into the family waiting room. My husband is walk-ing ahead of my nephews and the nurses who are consoling them; the doctor is coming out of my mother's room, again, and shaking his head from side to side as though he was in total disbelief. The doctor entered the room where we were asked to stay, and announced that he didn't know what had just happened, but Mrs. Jackson is ALIVE! And this time she is breathing on her own. There was no life support machine, or nothing hooked up to her. She just started breathing on her own. The entire room goes up in praises to the Lord. My husband ran out the room to meet the nephews to inform them of the good news. The two nurs-es that were helping to console my nephews fainted, collapsed when they heard the doctor, with the good news that she was back alive. The roles have now been reversed, my nephews are now trying to revive the nurses from their shocking experience. There was shouting going on all over that floor. Two elderly men were passing by to get into the elevator and asked what's going on down here— what's all the noise and commotion about? And a by-stander explained to the men that my mother had died but God saw fit to bring her back alive, and they began to shout, the elevator door closed before the two men were able to get on because the Holy Ghost was all over that place, they too started praising God. People in the hallways were seen shouting and clapping their hands as my hus-band returned to the room where I was still praising God for His goodness. I was shouting and praising the Lord as one of the hospital personnel was trying with all their might to calm me down, but to no avail, I had to give God all the glory, all the praise, and all the honor because I knew that it was His Grace and Mercy that brought her back to us, it was not her time to die. While I was still shout-ing and praising God for bringing my mother back to me, my husband asked the hospital staff to leave me alone while I was glorifying God and that I would be in the room to see my mother when the Holy Ghost permitted. I just didn't believe for one minute that God allowed me to drive fourteen hours to visit my mother, just for me to watch her die forty-five minutes after I had gotten there.

This whole scene happened so fast, it was about forty-five minutes from the time we entered the room until they came to tell us she was dead. I had never seen a place so filled with the Holy Spirit, as the hospital was that evening. We had one of the nurses to come up to us and said, "You are such a praying fam-ily and wondered if you could pray for me."

My mother lived twelve more hours before she actually died, God was preparing me for the worse because He knew that I couldn't have dealt with her death at that particular moment. In the wee hours in the morning, after suffering a massive heart attack, God called her to her Heavenly home. After eighty-one plus years, her living was definitely not in vain. Yes, she had done all she could do and beyond for her kids, grand kids and great grand kids. On her last day, last hour, God was still using my mother for His glory. She had made believers out of non-believers and reassured some of us who confess to believe that God is real and has all power in His all mighty hands!

At this point, I began to feel a whole lot like old man Job. Old man Job was a Servant of God. I felt like old man Job because God had taken my most precious jewel—my mother. At that moment, I truly felt as though I had lost everything I had; because, nothing else in this world really mattered to me anymore. "Though He slay me, yet will I trust him: but I will maintain mine own ways before him." Through all of my losses, trials and tribulations, I never complained or asked God why He quickly took so much from me. But, I must say, I did wonder what I could have done so badly to be thrown such a crooked, wicked curve ball. Then, I thought, God throws us curves too, just to keep us on the right path. I kept praying for strength and courage to continue on. God said that, "Man that is born of a woman is of few days, and full of trouble." All of us are going to have trouble in our life. We are going to have some good days, and we are going to have some bad days. Old man Job said, "death is inevitable" and that we must depart from this world. Life is like a shadow. When the sun goes down, what happens to the shadow? It goes away, it disappears."

Here, I will pause for a moment to give you just a little history on Old man Job so you'll see how I could compare my situation to his, and how I began to feel a lot like old man Job when my dear sister and my favorite uncle died, my mother's health failed her, and later losing my precious mother.

Old man Job was a rich man who lived in the land of Uz. He was a perfect and upright man. A man who was just minding his own business and trying to do right by everybody when he had a few unexpected guests to stop by his house to deliver him some bad news. Job is a man who experienced one situation after another situation—one trial after another. He had a visitor; I guess this is what you can call an unexpected guest—a messenger if you will, who came by to tell him that he had just lost all of his camels and asses. This is just like old Satan—his job is stealing, killing and destroying—now, here comes another unexpected messenger stopping by Job's house with more bad news, telling him that he had just lost all of his sheeps. Job's faith is still being tested—another messenger dropped by to tell him that he had lost all of his children. Job, himself, was also a very sick man. He was sick from his head to his feet but he never complained. He said, "The Lord giveth and the Lord taketh away." Through all of Job's suffering, he never sinned nor charged God foolishly. After all Job and his family had gone through, the devil is still at work, now here, his silly wife told him that he should just curse God and die—this is just like Satan. Also, his so-called friends turned their backs on him suggesting that he must have done something wrong for all of the suffering that he had encountered.

But, that is exactly what the devil wanted Job to think—put doubt in his mind. The devil wanted Job to feel like he had done something to deserve all the troubles that he went through, but Job maintained his integrity and his loyalty to God throughout all of his troubles.

I know another man, whose name is Jesus. He didn't complain either when the soldiers nailed His hands to the cross. They plaited a crown of thorns on His head. They speared Him in the side and blood and water ran down. They even hung Him out on Calvary, but He didn't complained. Jesus hung His head in the locks of His shoulder. Before His crucifixion, He was scourged, whipped, and beaten so badly that His flesh was wounded, cut and bruised which would cause the body to go into shock and hastened one's death. Still, Jesus didn't complain! But, He indicated pain and discomfort by saying, "I Thirst!" It is not that Jesus didn't suffer while He was on this earth, because He truly did suffer, but He did not complain. It was because of Jesus' suffering that all things were now accomplished that the scriptures might be fulfilled. Jesus' ministry was then completed. It was finished! At this point everything had been made perfect. Jesus didn't complain nor did He charge God for His suffering, but He did ask, "Father, forgive them; for they know not what they do." What an awesome God we serve!

After seeing all of what Job had lost, and then, all the things Jesus went through just for me so that I don't have to suffer, I won't complain nor will I charge Jesus for any of my suffering. Since I live by faith and not by sight, I had to continue to express unquenchable faith. However, when God took my mother, it appeared at times He had turned His back against me, I had to come to the realization that my mother is now a beautiful flower in God's garden. God loves beautiful flowers too.

In order for God to have a beautiful garden with a variety of flowers, He must pluck them from the earth. God has in His heavenly garden, flowers that hadn't yet blossom—they are still buds—these are His youth. Then, He has flowers that are in full blossom—they are strong and vibrant—these are His middle age. Then, He has flowers that have aged and withered, but by His grace and mercy, those flowers survived in this old wicked and evil world—these are His elderly, I continued to trust in Him and depend upon His Word because I know that God wouldn't leave me nor would He forsake me. He said that He would be with us until the end of the world. I thank God for choosing my mother to be a beautiful flower in His lovely garden. In God's lovely garden, there is nothing but joy, peace, love, patience, gentleness, goodness, faith, meekness, and temperance— oh, what a lovely garden to be planted in—singing in harmony—singing praises to God. It also states in 1st Samuel 2:33, "And the man of thine, whom I shall not cut off from mine altar, shall be to consume thine eyes, and to grieve thine heart: and all the increase of thine house shall die in the flower of their age."

It states in Luke chapter 17 that, *"If ye had faith as a grain of mustard seed, ye might say unto this sycamine tree Be thou plucked up by the root, and be thou planted in the sea; and it should obey you."*

Every time I think about God's garden of flowers, I think about how beautiful it must be; then, I smile because I know that my mother has a great, big smile on her face, proudly looking down on us, the seeds, the buds, the stems, and the flowers that she left behind, with her arms stretched wide opened, waiting to receive us in heaven.

CHAPTER THIRTEEN

FAITH: MY WALKING CANE TO GLORY

There is a spiritual hunger that rages within each of us that is very powerful but is not easily satisfied. We have a burning desire to know our purpose in life, and to have an intimate relationship and/or communion with God, the One who designed and made us—our whole body and soul.

To attain spiritual maturity, I urge you to develop enduring faith by seeking wisdom from God, and letting faith be your walking cane to glory. Faith is at work during all of our trials and tribulations. It is through our trials and tribulations that our faith is being tested. We are to accept our trials and tribulations with great joy and strength because of the good work God can and will accomplish through our test. God uses the most broken, bruised, and troubled people the most to do His will because they have been through the test and have become more mature as a result of their adversities.

Allowing God to lay His hands upon you and His plan to work in your life is, perhaps, just beginning to make its mark. The steep hill that you have been climbing for such a long, long time may be the ramp to a destiny beyond your imagination, hopes and dreams. Just hold on, and don't give up because the breakthrough that you have been asking for and long waiting for is just about to come. It's right around the corner.

We were all born for a reason. We all have a purpose in life, and our purpose must be guided with the help of the good Lord. We must remember that there is no such thing as birth by mistake, an accidental birth, or birth at the wrong time. Many have come and gone before you; and many will come and go after you, but it was in God's plans for you to be here at this time. Perhaps we are careless in our acts, but the children we borne as a result of our actions or our carelessness are by no means a mistakes—because God doesn't make mistakes. In spite of your brokenness, your hurts, and your insecurities, you were not an accident; you were destined to be just where you are today, and doing just the things that you are doing. However, God is not finished with you. He has a plan for your life, and you should be sick and tired of your situation that you are in, enough to want to change it because you are worthy of God's abundance—so, let God show you the Way.

God sends out His chosen messengers whom He hath trained in the boot camps and jungles of life only to release them with the gift of wisdom to bring forth His messages in order for those who are hungry for the knowledge of His Devine words may be fed, and to sing a new song in the congregation of Saints, to those who are eagerly seeking everlasting life. Faith, is believing in what you've never seen for greater is those who believe and have not seen and condemned are those who have seen and believe not. There is no way to the Father except through Jesus Christ. There is no way to Jesus except by Faith. There is no way to Faith except by believing.

Faith will restore marriages. Faith will transform prisoners to become law-abiding citizens. Faith will keep a roof over your head. Faith will keep food on your table. By having true faith is a life changing experience.

You may have spent many years indulging in self pity and anger; being very bitter, or holding a grudge against your birth mother; being prejudice and despising those around you because they are different than you; not liking who you are and battling to get out of your current situation; fighting the system and never becoming the person that God has destined for greatness. You can use all of your disappointments, your anger, your grudges and your fears to learn and grow from the various types of knowledge and experiences they bring—or you could use them to share with and help others as you become the person who God has brought forth with a unique plan that is part of His big master plan. You are destined for greatness in the fulfillment of that plan because God said in his Word that He gives us life, and that He gives it to us more abundantly. Allow faith to be your guide—to lead you throughout your life's journey. We should not subcome to the flesh lest we make ourselves slaves of it instead of servants of God.

When we are in a situation that we do not feel we should be, we must trust God to bring us out of it. Once God brings us out of the situation, we should not return to it, not forget what God has done for us. We should never forget our roots in our eternal, sovereign God. Weeping may endure for a night, but joy comes in the morning. And we will soon experience that morning in our lives when we should refuse to live the bitterness of our past. When we start trusting God and waiting on Him to bring us out of darkness and use us in His great plan, then we began to walk in the faith with confidence knowing that we are in union with the Lord.

Your dreams and fulfilling God's plan for your life may be delayed because of your circumstances or some small stumbling blocks; but don't ever let anyone stop you from pursuing and accomplishing your hopes and dreams. Keep the Faith and continue to seek that treasure stored especially for you. II Corinthians, 4:7-9 states, *"But we have this treasure in earthen vessels, that excellency of the power may be of God, and not of us. We are troubled on every side, yet not distressed; we are perplexed, but not in despair; persecuted, but not forsaken; cast down, but not destroyed."*

Also, remember that God has blessed us with skills that we have not yet tapped into. These skills are in our visions, dreams, and understandings. We need to know that the way to make it in this world is to use our intellectual ability that God has so graciously blessed us with. God gives to each of us a talent according to our own ability. It could be one talent it could be many talents. The one gift that He has given to all of us is to be able to spread His word and become humble servants in order to cure ourselves of the evils of the world and become successful with what is in store for us. Though our flesh is weak, we are blessed with a strong spirit because that is what truly belongs to God—He would not give us a weak spirit. When we subcome to the flesh, which is all around us, we join hands with Satan who is willing and able to toy with the weaknesses of the flesh, not our spirit, lest we be confused by him and not knowing the difference. Though Jesus is no longer of the flesh, He is still with us in the spirit, and we must keep watch with Him through our spirit and God will bless us through our faith and protect us from Satan with our comforter the "Holy Ghost." He alone is our "Walking Cane to Glory!" When we are in trouble, when we are in need, we call upon His name because we have the tool, "faith"—we say Jesus! Jesus! Jesus! Faith—even if it is the size of a little mustard seed. Trusting and believing God, hard work and perseverance will surely get us where we need to be in this life. With Christ Jesus, we have Victory over Satan everyday, and we don't ever want to become a quitter. Surely you have heard that old cliché, "A quitter never wins and a winner never quits." Quitting is what the devil wants us to do but with God, quitting is not even an option, as God wants us to conquer, to prosper and to develop into our full potential; and be all that we want to be, can be, and should be in Christ Jesus—to become the person of greatness.

Even if your dream seems impossible for you to obtain, have enough faith and believe that God is able to see you through it. We must learn to listen to the voice of God, who speaks to our soul, through our heart and spirit, then into our minds where lies the wisdom and understanding to know and interpret His message.

Just picture yourself doing whatever it is that you have always longed to do, being the kind of person you have always wanted to be—that's hoping and dreaming—and that is exactly what God wants us to do. God wants to make our goals and dreams come true, but we must have faith and listen to Him just as Daniel had too, as stated in the Bible. Daniel 10: 7-12, which states, *"And I Daniel alone saw the vision: for the men that were with me saw not the vision; but a great quaking fell upon them, so that they fled to hid themselves. Therefore I was left alone, and saw this great vision and there remained no strength in me: for my comeliness was turned in me into corruption, and I retained no strength. Yet heard I the voice of his words: and when I heard the voice of his words, then was I in a deep sleep on my face, and my face toward the ground. And, behold, a hand touched me, which set me upon my knees and upon the palms of my hands. And he said unto me, O Daniel, a man greatly beloved, understand the words that I speak unto thee, and stand upright: for unto thee am I now sent. And when he had spoken this word unto me, I stood trembling. Then said he unto me, Fear not, Daniel: for from the first day that thou didst set thine heart to understand, and to chasten thyself before thy God, thy words were heard, and I am come for thy words."*

When you see insurmountable stumbling blocks clouding your view, when you hear people say you don't have the skills, or maybe, the time isn't right—hold on. Perhaps, you lack boldness and courage as I did to keep on, keeping on. Maybe, you have children to raise; bills to pay like most of us do, and you get discouraged with yourself and God. If you feel it's too late to even think about pursuing your dreams because of age or economic condition—that's doubting and being fearful—and that's precisely what the devil wants you to do. Don't let the devil win. Don't let doubts and fears get in the way of your dreams. Don't let the people of the world pull down your courage. Let God be your "walking cane to glory." God wants us to know that we can do all things through Christ because He strengthens us to do it. The ones who keep their eyes fixed on the far target will get to it one day. The ones who keep Christ in their life and their eyes fixed on the prize will find his right road. You must be true to your highest aspirations, unrelenting; and you must be faithful to your dreams and to God. With Him as your walking cane, you will maximize your opportunities and minimize your obstacles. You will walk in the faith every day and never allow a setback of any kind to disrupt your dreams, overall plans and goals toward eternal life because failure is just a part of life and often a result of not trying hard enough or simply giving up. We fail because we are not obedient to the Word of God. It's not because of where we grew up, nor was it because whom we were raised by. It's simply because of our disobedience to God, and our attitude toward the situation. Our attitude causes us to fail and be defeated. God promotes only those that are faithful and can rise above their situation, their circumstances and their past. Once you've put your trust in our Father, the more you fail, the more you succeed if you keep trying because you learn from each failed attempt. Have Faith in God and allow His plan to lead and guide you through your life's journey. By putting God first, and with Him being in charge of your life, you are going to be successful in whatever direction you undertake because God will be ordering your steps. He will see that your dreams, goals, and aspirations are fulfilled. Having faith and believing in God is truly your walking cane to glory.

More importantly, you should constantly remind yourself that life is not a straight line from success to success but often two steps forward and one step backward. If you want to be a high achiever, have the ability and the courage to bounce back from defeat and take a step forward—one at a time. Anger and failure, even the bad and evil things in life, could be very positive, in that, it forces you to become very creative and strong. It also lights a fire underneath you that gives you the extra boost—the push you need to accomplish your goals, and overcome whatever obstacle Satan has lain in your path to make you stumble and fall, or stop trying.

Too often, too many people allow others to shape and influence their dreams and aspirations—their destiny. Don't accept society's judgment on who you are and what you will become or what you can accomplish in life because beside God, you are the only person who can put limitations on your potential—you are limited by your imagination not by how society judge you. If you let the world cast you into a role, you will never go beyond that role. If you let the world cast you down, you will get burned with no one to put the fire out lest you fall to your knees for God's grace and mercy.

Make your own definition in life of who you are and what you will become or what you can accomplish. Success is a journey not a destination, and we have the wisdom to understand all things through the Holy Spirit which cometh from the wisest of us all.

If you are drawn to be successful at whatever God has planned for you, you will eventually come to know what it is in spite of the hurdles put before you. Remember also that hurdles to success are most easily overcome when people take responsibility for their own lives, their actions and successes. Always honor and respect your personality and your temperament. Respond to the inner voice that is calling you to move in a specific direction. God wants us to obey His will and He will provide our needs. When the Lord comes, He should find us serving Him, _"But of that day and hour knoweth no man, no, not the angels of heaven, but my Father only."_ Matthew 24:36. _"For the Kingdom of heaven is as a man traveling into a far off country."_

Furthermore, when things don't work out the way we expect them too, and life becomes discouraging, the best antidote lies in maintaining a good sense of humor. A good sense of humor is essential for a balanced life as joy comes through the soul. The ability to laugh at yourself, at your disappointments, and at your circumstances ensures that you are not taking your failures too seriously. Also, humor pushes back feelings of depression and discouragement, making room for creativity, innovative thoughts, commitment and peace within our hearts and souls.

Often when we seek to make the right choices in life, we are encountered by trials and tribulations that test our faith in the Almighty and leave us to the exposure of evaluating our own self-worth. But, as we become determined and destined for spiritual change, we must surround ourselves with the comforter—the Holy Ghost, in order to gain salvation over Satan, and as we start counting our blessings and soaring to new heights. After coming to a fork in the road, we must edify ourselves in the glorious power of God. Have faith in Him and reap the rewards of that faith, then, if we fail to feed the faith and keep the faith, we are destined to perish without it.

Finally, remember to adequately plan, set realistic goals and practice perseverance. Victory belongs to the most persevering. Also, remember that the only real failure in life is failing to move forward, to move in the direction of your dreams. The most common threat to life is that we waste too much of it on trivial and meaningless pursuits. In order to rise above your assumptions, you need to challenge them, and have faith in the almighty powers of God. The bible tells us that the race is not given to the swift, but it is given to the ones who endure until the end. By following God's plan for your life, you have the power to shape your destiny because destiny is no more than a matter of choice than a chance, and you already have the gift of choosing, the right to choose, the freedom to choose because you are allowed too, by the generosity of our Heavenly Father.

On 2 January 1998, approximately 7:45 P.M., while sitting in the den of my home, in Montgomery, Alabama, with my husband, right in the midst of our conversation, an overwhelming feeling came over me...at that moment, through the Holy Spirit, the title of the book was conceived. The words just started flowing. The Holy Spirit has led me to share with others some of my life experiences, my beliefs and Faith in God in hopes that it will encourage others to trust, believe and have Faith in our all mighty God, and to allow Him to be their walking cane to glory. God is real.

You have just experienced traveling on a journey with me, through your conscious and the spirit that dwells within you. You've also read all about faith, and how faith could be your "walking cane to glory." Faith: A Walking Cane to Glory! We must remember that Jesus is the walking cane that we need to get to glory. Faith is the key to obtain the Cane we need to began our journey to glory, and He came to earth for each and everyone of us, and we know not the time or place when He will return—just be ready to go with Him when He comes back for us. We are all on the earth for just a short while to love, to be loved, to reproduce, and to seek the eternal Kingdom of God. Why not allow the wisdom which life has taught us—be it through overcoming tribulations and obstacles in gaining this understanding—why not let God be our walking cane through this life's journey. We cannot travel this road alone as it is too filled with events and people who will try to stop us—stop us from being successful in this life as we are being successful in walking in the faith until we cross over to the other side where eternal life shall be realized, and ours to gain and hope for. Therefore, God is watching and guiding His children and servants who seek first His Kingdom. Jesus taught the truth after God had sent Him to the earth so that we can all come to know the power of God, who is the God of the living. We must surrender ourselves to Him in order to receive His full blessings, and surrender the things that we try to hold onto that are not ours to have. God doesn't need faith because He is faith. Let go, and let God be your walking cane to glory. Matthew 22:21 states, *"Render therefore to Caesar the things which are Caesar's; and unto God the things that are God's."*

Of all the tragedies and losses in my life, I gave up the search and found myself. Now, that I have my life back, I'm free to love and to write again. Thank God for being my walking cane because, without Him, I wouldn't be able to continue on this path—this life's journey. Writing this book for me has been both very exhilarating and exhausting; but I don't feel no ways tire because God didn't bring me this far to leave me. I come too far from where I started from to go back. When I learned and understood the Love that God had for me, I knew that I had to press my way; because He loved me so much.

Thank you Jesus for making this all possible and being my "Walking Cane" throughout my life's journey!

As I come to a close with my writing, I would like to share the following poem with you to show you just how much God Loves you. Because He loved you so much and because He died for you, why don't you make a choice to live for Him? Enjoy!

A LOVE STORY

One day, I woke early in the morning to watch the sunrise.
Ah the beauty of God's creation is beyond description.
As I watched, I praised God for His beautiful work.
As I sat there, I felt the Lord's presence with me.

He asked me, "Do you love me?"
I answered, "Of course, God! You are my Lord and Savior!"
Then He asked, "If you were physically handicapped, would you still love me?"
I was perplexed. I looked down upon my arms, legs and the rest of my body and wondered how many things I wouldn't be able to do, the things that I took for granted. And I answered, "It would be tough Lord, but I would still love You."

Then the Lord said, "If you were blind, would you still love my creation?"
How could I love something without being able to see it?
Then I thought of all the blind people in the world and how many of them still loved God and His creation. So I answered, "It's hard to think of it, but I would still love you."
The Lord then asked me, "If you were deaf, would you still listen to my word?"

How could I listen to anything being deaf? Then I understood.
Listening to God's Word is not merely using our ears, but our hearts.
I answered, "It would be tough, but I would still listen to Your word."

The Lord then asked, "If you were mute, would you still praise My Name?"
How could I praise without a voice?
Then it occurred to me: God wants us to sing from our very heart and soul. It never matters what we sound like. And praising God is not always with a song, but when we are persecuted, we give God praise with our words of thanks.

So I answered, "Though I could not physically sing, I would still praise Your Name."

And the Lord asked, "Do you really love Me? With courage and a strong conviction?"

I answered boldly, "Yes Lord! I love You because You are the one and true God!"

I thought I had answered well, but...

God asked,

"THEN WHY DO YOU SIN?"

I answered, "Because I am only human. I am not perfect."

"THEN WHY IN TIMES OF PEACE DO YOU STRAY THE FURTHEST? WHY ONLY IN TIMES OF TROUBLE DO YOU PRAY THE EARNEST?"

No answers. Only tears.

The Lord continued:

"Why only sing at fellowships and retreats?
Why seek Me only in times of worship?
Why ask things so selfishly?
Why ask things so unfaithfully?"
The tears continued to roll down my cheeks.
"Why are you ashamed of Me?
Why are you not spreading the good news?
Why in times of persecution, you cry to others when I offer you My
*   shoulder to cry on?*
Why make excuses when I give you opportunities to serve in My
*   Name?"*

I tried to answer, but there was no answer to give.

"You are blessed with life. I made you not to throw this gift away.
I have blessed you with talents to serve Me, but you continue to turn away.
I have revealed My Word to you, but you do not gain in knowledge.
I have spoken to you but your ears were closed.
I have shown My blessings to you, but your eyes were turned away.
I have sent you servants, but you sat idly by as they were pushed away.
I have heard your prayers and I have answered them all."

"DO YOU TRULY LOVE ME ?"

I could not answer. How could I? I was embarrassed beyond belief.

I had no excuse. What could I say to this?
When my heart had cried out and the tears had flowed, I said,
"Please forgive me Lord. I am unworthy to be Your child."
The Lord answered, "That is My Grace, My Child." I asked,
"Then why do you continue to forgive me? Why do You love me
so?"

The Lord answered,

" Because you are My Creation. You are my Child. I will never abandon you.

>   *When you cry, I will have compassion and cry with you.*
>   *When you shout with joy, I will laugh with you.*
>   *When you are down, I will encourage you.*
>   *When you fall, I will raise you up.*
>   *When you are tired, I will carry you.*
>   *I will be with you till the end of days, and I will love you forever."*

Never had I cried so hard before. How could I have been so cold?
How could I have hurt God as I had done?

I asked God, "How much do You love me?"

The Lord stretched out His arms, and I saw His nail-pierced hands. I
bowed down at the feet of Christ, my Savior. And for the first time, I
truly prayed.

Author Unknown.

*The words in this poem are very special, and they deserve to be
shared. Don't just read this and forget about it, use it in your everyday
life, and know that God truly loves you. Use God in your life, and in
your everyday plan. Always remember God loves US all...God Bless!*

GOING TO THE THRONE OF GRACE

In the book of Luke, God said, when you pray, say, Our Father which art in Heaven, Hollowed be thy name. Thy kingdom comes. Thy will be done, as in heaven, so in earth. Give us this day our daily bread. And forgive us our sins; for we also forgive every one that is indebted to us. And lead us not into temptation; but deliver us from evil. Lord, I come to you once more and again with thanksgiving in my heart. Thanking and praising you for Your goodness. We thank You for the Holy Spirit leading and guiding us that we might walk righteously. I pray that you heal all sickness that is amongst us, in the name of Jesus. Father, You said in Your word that You were bruised for our iniquity, wounded for our transgression, the chastisement for our peace was upon You and by Your stripes, we are healed. We thank You for Your healing power, in the name of Jesus. We ask that you comfort the bereaved families everywhere. Let them know Father that they are not alone, and that You are with them now and until the end of the world. You said in Your word that You would not leave us nor would you forsake us. Lord, we thank you for the love that you have shown us down through the years. You showed us the love that you have for us when You were nailed to the cross, and died for us so that we could have a chance to the tree of life. We thank you for Joy; because the Joy of the Lord is our strength and it should come every morning that we awaken by your grace and mercy. We thank You for Grace and Mercy.

We thank you for new anointing and new grace each and everyday. Lord, I thank You for being my shepherd. Lord, as long as I know that You are my shepherd, I shall not want for a thing. I come asking for peace all over the world today, in the name of Jesus. I know Father that You said in Your Word that if we seek Your face, pray and turn from our wicked ways, then will You hear from Heaven and heal the land. Lord, help us to seek Your face in the name of Jesus; so that we can have peace. We thank you for hope today. Someone is about to let go of their hopes, their dreams, and even their life because they feel that they just don't have the strength to go on any longer or any further. Father, we stand in the gap for them today. We are holding-on in their stead, in hopes that they may see Your good works in us, and grab hold of Your goodness, and make that change in their lives and come on over to your side, so that we can live the life that You have planned for them. Satan doesn't want us to enjoy the blessings that You have given us, and this is just another opportunity in our life to show

You, no matter what, that we do have Faith in YOU—our eternal God, that You will come through for us—not matter what. Thank You Jesus!

Lord, I want to take this moment to offer salvation to the lost. If there is anyone out there that hadn't accepted Christ in their lives, this is your chance, your moment. If I were you, I wouldn't take too long to make up my mind; because time is running out. Where would your home be if God called you home right now—where will it be? Would it be Heaven or would it be Hell? Father, You said in your words that if anyone confesses with there mouth that Jesus is Lord; and believe in their heart that God raised Jesus from the dead shall be saved. I pray this prayer in the name of Jesus. Amen!

ABOUT THE AUTHOR

DeLois Jackson is a native Floridian. She is an employee of the Federal Government. She enjoys writing, reading, walking, traveling and spending time with her lovely grandchildren. She graduated from Troy State University, in 1986, with a Bachelor of Science in Business Management. In 1994, she received her Master of Science in Human Resource Management.

DeLois is currently the President of her Toastmasters club, and she is an active member of the Americans Business Women Association. She is a member of Greater Galilee Baptist Church. She is very compassionate and considerate of people that she comes in contact with. She is always encouraging and uplifting people who are around her, to let go, and let God be their walking cane to glory. She has spoken to various groups. She was a member of the Prison Outreach Ministry and Co-Youth Director at her church. She has witnessed the goodness of God to numerous age groups. She has experienced the miraculous works of the Lord, and knows the value of having intimacy with and humility before God. She has three lovely daughters: Tonya, Adora and NaKisha. She and her husband are currently residing in Fairborn, Ohio.